D1601520

ALSO BY RICHARD FOSTER
The Real Bettie Page: The Truth About the Queen of the Pinups
(*Kensington Publishing*)

PRAISE FOR *THE REAL BETTIE PAGE*:
"What was the dark secret of Bettie Page – the curvaceous black-banged pinup goddess who titillated 1950s America with S&M poses, abandoned her career in 1957, and disappeared? ... Journalist [Richard] Foster, in this sensationalistic, albeit scrupulously researched book, reveals that in 1979 and 1982, Page (a diagnosed schizophrenic) tried to stab several people to death and was institutionalized. ... An eloquent fan, he brings ... insight into her recent revival as a sex symbol."

– Entertainment Weekly

Southern Nightmare: The Hunt for the South Side Strangler

RICHARD FOSTER

Southern Nightmare: The Hunt for the South Side Strangler
by Richard Foster

Published by True South Media LLC, Midlothian, VA

www.SouthernNightmare.com

© 2018 True South Media LLC

For permissions contact:
info@southernnightmare.com

10 9 8 7 6 5 4 3 2 1

Library of Congress Control Number: 2018911109

ISBN: 978-0-692-19354-9 (paperback)
ISBN: 978-0-692-19069-2 (ebook)

Cover by Miriam Foster

Southern Nightmare logo design by Ed Harrington;
photo by Kent Eanes for *Style Weekly* magazine

DEDICATION

This book is dedicated to the memories and families of Carolyn Hamm, Debbie Davis, Dr. Susan Hellams, Diane Cho and Sue Tucker.

You are not forgotten.

CONTENTS

ACKNOWLEDGMENTS

I n working on this project, I was fortunate to receive support and assistance from many individuals and media partners, including *Style Weekly* magazine, WRIR 97.3 FM Richmond Independent Radio, Sound of Music Studios and PEN America. I'm also very grateful for the partnership (and patience) of my wife, Miriam Foster, who handled the design and layout for this book, as well as our *Southern Nightmare* website and social media content. *Style Weekly*'s multitalented art director Ed Harrington designed the *Southern Nightmare* series logo. (You can disappear down an Instagram rabbit hole checking out Ed's twisted comic takes on pop culture iconography @nothinghappenedtoday.) And the podcast could not have happened without the hard work and care of our extraordinarily gifted studio producer and friend John Morand at Sound of Music.

I conducted more than 50 interviews for *Southern Nightmare* over a roughly 10-month period, speaking with sources ranging from friends, family and co-workers of the South Side Strangler's victims to retired homicide detectives, prosecutors, FBI agents, defense attorneys and forensic science experts. Everyone was exceedingly generous with their time.

I will remain forever thankful to Judy McCloskey, Eric and Judy Fiske, Hyun Kyung Cho, Roman Cho and Reg Tucker for their trust and graciousness in sharing their memories, both cherished and painful, of the loved ones who were taken from them. I'd also like to extend special thanks to retired Arlington County homicide detective

Joe Horgas, retired Richmond city homicide detective Ray Williams, former Arlington County Commonwealth's Attorney Helen Fahey and defense attorneys Carl Womack, Jeff Everhart and Dave Johnson for providing firsthand accounts of what it was like to be at the center of this maelstrom.

I'm also indebted to Dr. Marcella Fierro, Billy Davenport, Art Karp, Larry McCann, Steve Mardigian, Judd Ray, Kenneth E. Melson, Dr. Harold Young and Louis Schlesinger, as well as Jeffrey Ban, Brad Jenkins, and Katya Herndon from the Virginia Department of Forensic Science, and many others too numerous to mention for their kindness in making time to talk with me for this project. I also need to thank all my media colleagues who gave me advice and encouragement as I worked on *Southern Nightmare*, including Lori Collier Waran, Lisa Antonelli Bacon, Lorna Wyckoff, Jack Cooksey, Carol Olson and Gary Harki.

And I must acknowledge the source materials used in researching this book. In addition to the many interviews I conducted, I also consulted contemporaneous reporting from the *Richmond Times-Dispatch* and WRVA 1140 AM via the Library of Virginia's archives. I am also grateful to Carl Womack for the loan of court records and transcripts from the Arlington trial. Books that provided a wealth of information and leads for me included Paul Mones' 1995 nonfiction account, *Stalking Justice: The Dramatic True Story of the Detective Who First Used DNA Testing to Catch a Serial Killer*, as well as the 2008 law-enforcement textbook *Serial Violence: Analysis of Modus Operandi and Signature Characteristics of Killers (Practical Aspects of Criminal and Forensic Investigations)(First Ed.)* by Robert D. Keppel and William J. Birnes.

Finally, I want to thank all of the *Southern Nightmare*'s podcast listeners for making this project such a success. Watching your ranks grow and grow each week was a real joy and receiving your positive support and feedback sustained me through the busiest, craziest, most exhausting summer of my life. You all have my sincere gratitude.

– *Richard Foster, September 2018*

INTRODUCTION

Thirty years ago, the South Side Strangler stalked the streets of Richmond, Virginia, raping and murdering women in their homes and terrorizing the entire city.

This case marked a milestone in U.S. history: the first time a murderer would be brought to justice using DNA evidence. And that murderer just so happened to be a serial killer who had haunted my hometown when I was a teen.

This is not only a gripping, epic true-crime tale but it's probably one of the most important chapters in the history of forensic science and the modern American criminal justice system. It set the stage for how police use DNA to catch killers today. And chances are good you've never even heard about it.

From 1997 to 1999, I was a full-time staff writer at *Style Weekly* magazine, the city's alternative weekly tabloid. Not long after I joined *Style*, one of my co-workers mentioned that the South Side Strangler's first victim, Debbie Davis, had also worked at *Style*. Her murder had happened 10 years prior and there were still several people there who had worked with Debbie. It had been a dark time for *Style* and Richmond.

Last year, in 2017, I entered into a partnership with *Style* to create a podcast and an accompanying series of articles about the 30th anniversary of the South Side Strangler case.

That became the *Southern Nightmare* podcast, which told the entire chilling saga in sequence over 10 episodes. Since the podcast launched in May 2018, it has attracted listeners in all 50 states and more than 95 nations. It briefly cracked the U.S. iTunes Top 100 podcast chart and climbed to No. 11 on the Australian charts. As of September 2018, it has been downloaded around 225,000 times.

Recently one of our listeners tweeted that as she listened to the final episode, she realized that the entire series had been a love letter to forensic science and DNA testing. I would agree and also add that it's combined with some small measure of pride at the many talented professionals from my home state of Virginia who helped shape the modern future of forensic science and criminal investigations.

It is really difficult to understate how groundbreaking the South Side Strangler case was in 1988. Before this, dusting for fingerprints and comparing blood types were still the best ways to link a criminal to a crime.

Today, everyone knows about DNA. But this happened way before the O.J. Simpson trial or TV shows like *CSI* and *NCIS* popularized the idea that police can use genetic testing to catch killers. It was even years before *Jurassic Park* – both the Michael Crichton novel _and_ the blockbuster Spielberg movie.

I began working on *Southern Nightmare* in fall 2017 and I interviewed more than 50 people for this project, including homicide detectives, FBI profilers, prosecutors, defense attorneys and friends and family of the victims.

The culmination of that work is this book, which includes extra material we didn't have time to get into in the 30-minute podcast episodes. It clarifies some things, corrects a few unintentional factual errors and generally provides additional context – along with adding in some new reporting and research.

As you read this book, you'll hear about how homicide detectives and prosecutors desperately worked behind the scenes to stop this serial killer before he could kill again. You'll find out how the South Side Strangler became the first murderer in American history to be caught via DNA. You'll also learn how this case changed the nature of law enforcement investigation work across the nation … and how it led to freeing a wrongly convicted man.

Most importantly, you'll hear the stories of the women killed by the South Side Strangler as told by their family and friends. In a lot of true-crime books and TV shows, murder victims are reduced to plot points – like Mr. Boddy in the *Clue* board game. They're not treated like real people. This book aims to do better.

Over 30 years, some memories may have faded but the pain of these murders still echoes on in the people who knew and loved these women and they deserve not to be forgotten.

Remember their names: Carolyn Hamm, Debbie Davis, Dr. Susan Hellams, Diane Cho and Sue Tucker.

Because of their deaths, others are alive.

CHAPTER 1

THE EMPTY CAR

The car had been running all night.

When Richmond, Virginia, mechanic Arnold Ellis woke up that Saturday morning on September 19, 1987, the little white 1985 Renault Alliance that had been parked in front of his Forest Hill Avenue house was still sitting in the same spot. It'd been there when he'd arrived home around 1 a.m. after attending an American Legion dance and he thought it was a little suspicious. People didn't usually park there because Forest Hill Avenue is a busy roadway on the city's South Side. Now, more than six hours later in the bright morning daylight, Ellis was able to discern that the car's engine was running – had it been on all night? The keys were in the ignition and there was no sign of the car's driver.

Assuming the abandoned vehicle had probably been stolen, Ellis called the police. Richmond patrol officer Lyle Harding responded to the call later that morning. After running the plates with the state Department of Motor Vehicles, he learned the car was registered to a Debbie Dudley Davis, age 35, who lived about one street north and a few blocks west on the ground floor of a large, World War-II-era brick apartment building on Devonshire Street, right near the sprawling Forest Hill Park.

"Well," Harding told Ellis, "let me go see if this young lady knows where her car is."

At around 9:30 a.m. Harding drove to the building and knocked on Davis' door but no one answered. Alerted by the commotion, an elderly neighbor came out and gave the officer her set of spare keys to Debbie Davis' apartment.

Inside, the patrolman would find a nightmare that would haunt and terrify Richmond for months to come.

Debbie Davis' dead body was lying face down across her bed, her head hanging slightly over the side. She was topless, wearing only a pair of cutoff blue jeans shorts. Her right arm was tied tightly behind her back with thick bootlaces; her left arm was tied beneath her. The killer had tightly wrapped a thick, dark navy blue woolen sock around her neck, using a 16-inch metal tube attachment from her vacuum cleaner to ratchet the sock clockwise like a tourniquet. Knotted at the front of her throat, the taut sock resembled a macabre bow. (Medical examiners would be forced to cut it loose with scissors, causing a popping sound. The metal vacuum cleaner cylinder had been twisted at least two to three times, causing the rope-like wool sock to slice through the muscles of her neck and into her larynx and voice box.)

The whites of Davis' open eyes were dotted red from ruptured blood vessels, a telltale sign of prolonged strangulation.

Above the kitchen sink in Davis's apartment, the window and screen were open about 12 inches. A rocking chair the killer had stolen from a porch a block away was leaned against the outside wall beneath the window, bearing silent witness to how the intruder had entered – and exited – the apartment. The window sill had been a good eight feet above the ground, so the killer had to pull himself up and through the window. The feat would have required some significant upper body strength.

Inside, below the window, sitting on the kitchen counter to the right of the sink, were two glasses, a glazed ceramic vase holding kitchen utensils and a full, two-liter bottle of generic diet soda. On the opposite side of the sink, an empty Cool-Whip container Debbie

Davis had been using as Tupperware sat in the light blue plastic drying rack. The murderer had obviously taken care not to disturb any of the items around the sink on the way in or out.

The patrol officer secured the scene and radioed in the murder.

Richmond Homicide Detective Ray Williams was downtown on East Main Street, about 10 minutes away, when he got the call. He'd already been a homicide detective for 13 years and he'd worked some of the city's biggest murder cases but even he was taken aback by the crime scene he found in Debbie Davis' bedroom.

"My first thought was this is unusual. We never had a homicide like this. And then I knew it's going to be tough," recalls Williams, who's been retired for almost 20 years. "You think a regular murder's tough? Try one of these."

The killer entered Debbie Davis' apartment via this kitchen window, leaving all items on the sink undisturbed.

This would be the first murder in Richmond committed by a serial killer who would come to be known as the South Side Strangler. Before it was over, he would terrorize two Virginia cities 100 miles apart while homicide detectives, prosecutors and FBI prosecutors raced to stop him.

The series of horrific murders would go on to become a landmark case in the history of the American criminal justice system: the first time in U.S. history that a killer had been sentenced to death based of DNA evidence. And that murderer just happened to be a serial killer.

Summer 2018 marked the 30th anniversary of this milestone case, which happened almost seven years before the O.J. Simpson trial and long before television series like *CSI: Crime Scene Investigation* and *NCIS* would popularize the idea of using DNA as a criminal investigation tool.

It was the last weekend of summer 1987. That Saturday morning car radios could be heard playing the latest No. 1 pop music hit, "I Just Can't Stop Loving You," the first single off Michael Jackson's new album, *Bad*. The film *Fatal Attraction*, starring Michael Douglas and Glenn Close, had just premiered in theaters the night before.

Lorna Wyckoff was at her home on Richmond's fashionable Monument Avenue in the city's Fan District, packing for a short trip. Wyckoff was the founder and publisher of *Style Weekly*, the city's scrappy, popular alternative weekly news magazine. She had laid out the tabloid's first issue on her kitchen table in 1982; five years later, *Style Weekly* magazine had dozens of employees on the payroll, all working out of a spacious, three-story old brownstone on the edge of nearby Virginia Commonwealth University's urban campus.

There was a knock at Wyckoff's front door. Waiting on her stoop were two Richmond homicide detectives: Ray Williams and Glenn Williams. Though they had attended high school together, Ray and Glenn weren't related. But everybody called them the Williams Boys just the same.

Sandy haired, on the short side and stocky with boyish good looks, Ray was in his mid-30s and was both book-smart and street-smart, thanks to his hard upbringing in Richmond's tough, working-class Oregon Hill neighborhood. Glenn, who was taller and larger, was a bear of a man with a receding hairline and a full, black beard. He was little quieter, a little more down-to-earth, happy to let Ray take the lead and be the center of attention.

The Williams Boys asked Wyckoff if Debbie Davis was one of her employees.

"I said yes and was told that she had been murdered," Wyckoff recalls. "It was something out of a movie. ... I think I fainted."

Debbie had worked as *Style*'s accounts manager for two years.

Just before seeing Wyckoff, the two detectives had paid a visit to Debbie's cousin, Judy Maybeury Fiske, and her husband, Eric. The couple and their two young sons lived in the South Side neighborhood of Westover Hills, just a block and a half from Debbie's Forest Hill apartment. Judy and Debbie had grown up together and were best friends.

"You don't ever forget it," remembers Judy, the minister of worship and music at the city's Tabernacle Baptist Church.

"It was a Saturday morning. We were out working in the yard," recalls Eric Fiske, now a retired senior assistant state attorney general.

The Williams Boys walked up and asked the Fiskes if they were related to Debbie Davis.

"It was like, uhhh, this is not good. So you know something terrible has gone on," recalls Judy.

Eric phoned Debbie's father, Bill Dudley, who hung up on Eric when he was told what happened. "Bill just was devastated," Eric says.

"She was their life," says Judy. "She was their only child. She was very much daddy's girl. It was real hard for him. It was real hard for both of them."

❖

Debbie Davis was born and raised in Campbell County, just outside Lynchburg, Virginia, a small-town, conservative city best known as the home base of the late televangelist and Moral Majority leader the Rev. Jerry Falwell, who founded Thomas Road Baptist Church and Liberty University there. It's about a two-hour drive west from Richmond, the state capital. Debbie grew up there playing with her cousin Judy, who was around the same age. The two girls were like sisters.

"There were always dogs and cats and stuff around and we spent a lot of time out at her place basically just kind of playing with [her] backyard horse," Judy says, reminiscing. "We just fooled around and played with horses and played with dolls and did what kids do."

Every Sunday afternoon, the girls would visit their grandmother's farm about 40 minutes away in rural Appomattox County "to have lunch with Grandma ... and we played in the woods and ran around on the farm and shucked corn and played with cows."

**Debbie Davis at her parents' home near
Lynchburg, Virginia, 1980s** *(family photo)*

After graduating from Brookville High School in 1970, Debbie entered into a brief marriage that ended in divorce. She spent her 20s as an office worker for a moving company. In the early 1980s, Debbie moved to Richmond to be closer to Judy, who lived south of the James River in Westover Hills, a quiet, middle-class community of tidy brick Cape Cods, ranchers and two-story homes built from the 1920s through the 1960s.

"The thing I remember most about Debbie was her laugh," recalls Eric, whose two young sons knew his wife's cousin as Aunt Debbie. "She had such a great laugh. I [also] loved her honesty."

"She'd didn't pull any punches," Judy agrees, laughing.

"I mean, if she thought you did something stupid, she didn't hesitate to tell you that really was stupid," Eric says.

"And if your dress was ugly, it was just ugly," says Judy, chuckling. "Like, you *really* shouldn't wear that."

Debbie enjoyed life in Richmond and "she loved *Style*. She was really excited to work at *Style*," Judy recalls. "She'd worked for moving companies since she graduated high school, so it was a really different atmosphere. And she loved entertainment and she loved movies and she liked being where the action is."

Style Weekly, which built its early reputation reporting on local restaurants and the arts, was a perfect fit for Debbie, a pop-culture fan who enjoyed reading mystery novels and listening to Bruce Springsteen records. She could walk from her apartment to the nearby Westover Hills movie theater.

Debbie Davis also worked part-time selling books at the Waldenbooks store at nearby Cloverleaf Mall.

In addition to her full-time job as the accounts manager for *Style*, Debbie worked a night or two a week as a sales clerk at the Waldenbooks store at Chesterfield County's Cloverleaf Mall, which was also on the South Side, about a 10-minute drive west from her apartment. Built in 1972, Cloverleaf was one of the area's top three large indoor malls, anchored by Sears and J.C. Penney department stores and a local upscale retailer, Thalhimer's.

Style Weekly founder Lorna Wyckoff hired Debbie Davis and remembers those days fondly: "It really was like a big garage band of people who had good intentions – not really a lot of knowledge, but we would figure it out. And Debbie was the house mother. She was the person who always had these little bowls of candy on her desk.

"She was warm and friendly, a good worker. She was just kind of a salt-of-the-earth woman. She liked to read, so she was always reading the latest paperback or bestseller. I remember we were both enchanted with John le Carré, whodunits and detectives and spies, and, to me, it would turn out very ironic that Patsy Cornwell's first major hit, *Postmortem*, was based on Debbie's life. It was bizarre poetic injustice."

One of Debbie's jobs as *Style*'s accounts manager was handling the magazine's collectibles and past-due payments from advertisers, "of which there were many," Wyckoff says, "and she really made it into sort of a fun thing, going after this restaurant owner who hadn't paid in months. And she was dogged. She would track him down. She would find him, she would call him, she would stay on it and happily come back and high-five with me that she'd gotten at least gotten $50 out of a $400 receivable or something like that."

The night before her murder, Debbie and a co-worker, Deona Landes Houff, left *Style* early and took a road trip to Virginia Beach to see a live stand-up comedy performance by *Saturday Night Live* star Dana Carvey, who at the time was best known for his breakout Church Lady character.

Rushed for time because they wanted to stroll on the beach before the show, the two women left money on the table at the restaurant where they ate dinner, instead of waiting for the check.

"They were annoyed with us because they knew we were leaving. [But] we left cash," Houff says with a shrug, laughing. "It was important to us to walk on the beach and I'm very glad we did – based on what happened, of course."

Later that night, back in Richmond, Houff dropped Debbie off at her apartment, waiting to drive away until Debbie was safely inside.

Davis lived in a ground-floor apartment (*far left*) in this World War II-era building bordering the Forest Hill and Westover Hills neighborhoods on the South Side of Richmond. Her body was wheeled down this sidewalk on a stretcher while police spoke with local TV news reporters.

"I remember seeing her. I could see her hand. You know how you wave out the window? 'Yeah, I'm in, I'm fine,'" Houff recalls. "And of course later I remember wondering, god, was he watching that happen? Did he watch me drop her off that night? Because I think they thought he watched. He knew who she was."

"I would say he watched each of them for more than five days," says Ray Williams, the retired homicide detective. "He would make sure that nobody was there with them."

The night of her murder, Debbie was tired and not feeling well, suffering from abdominal cramps.

Earlier in the week, she called her friend and coworker, *Style Weekly* art director Kent Eanes, in the middle of the night and asked him to pick her up and take her to the emergency room. The doctors told Debbie she needed to get her gallbladder removed soon. Between the medicine she was taking for the pain and getting home late from her road trip to Virginia Beach the night before, she was feeling a little wiped out. When she left work that day, she told Lorna she was going to curl up in bed with a book and hit the sack early.

On the evening of Friday, September 18, 1987, Eric Fiske walked over to Debbie's apartment with his young sons, then ages 1 and 3, so they could visit with their Aunt Debbie, like they often did. He pulled his infant son behind him in a red Radio Flyer wagon.

Eric knew that Debbie wasn't going home to visit her parents that weekend because she was feeling ill. "She didn't want to get the boys sick, so we stood outside her window and spoke to her through the window," he recalls. "It was probably about 7:30 at night. And that was the last time we saw her."

Eric Fiske and his sons were likely the last people – apart from the killer – to see Debbie Davis alive. At that point, she probably had less than four hours to live.

Around 8:30 p.m. she called her parents, Bill and Josie Dudley. Bill had come to Richmond earlier in the week to carry Debbie to the hospital for a sonogram following her emergency room visit and they were discussing when Debbie would be coming to Lynchburg to get the gallbladder operation she needed. Her parents planned to take care of her while she recovered. They also chatted about their weekend plans and Debbie told them she was going shopping in the morning.

After about an hour, Bill and Josie Dudley said goodbye to their daughter, never realizing it was for the final time.

"The last thing she said was, 'Daddy, go ahead and retire, and do it now,'" Bill Dudley told local newspaper the *Richmond Times-Dispatch*, in May 1989. "That was the last thing I heard her say on the telephone."

The South Side Strangler was already inside Debbie's apartment, listening to the entire conversation.

"I think he was hiding in the hallway closet," says Ray Williams. "Her eyeglasses were in the hallway; so was [her] toothbrush. She was probably going to the bathroom to brush her teeth when he grabbed her."

Debbie Davis, circa 1984 (*family photo*)

When police found her body the next morning, the latest bestseller, mystery novelist Scott Turow's debut book, *Presumed Innocent*, was resting on Debbie's nightstand next to a drinking glass still half-filled with diet soda. Eerily prescient, the novel's plot revolved around a bondage murder. A few years later it would be adapted into a movie starring Harrison Ford.

"It was sitting right on her nightstand where she'd been reading it," Ray says in the raspy Southern twang of a native Richmonder who was once a three-pack-a-day Marlboro reds smoker. A quadruple bypass survivor, these days the 68-year-old former homicide detective relies on a portable, battery-powered pump to keep his heart beating. It doesn't keep him from playing racquetball with friends or driving in his pristine black 1979 Corvette, though.

As murder scenes go, Debbie Davis' bedroom was virtually bloodless and clean. A row of stuffed animals on a dresser blindly smiled out at the detectives, ignorant of the horrors that had taken place there. A nearby ironing board stood undisturbed with Debbie's work clothes casually draped over it, just as she had left them there after changing the previous night.

There were no fingerprints. Nothing had been taken, as far as investigators could tell. Her purse still money inside it. There were no witnesses and no obvious suspects. None of her neighbors heard a thing.

"No hair, no fibers, no fingerprints. We knew he was smart. Very seldom does a crook do that kind of damage and spend that much time with his victim and not leave a bunch of clues. But he left nothing," Williams says, recalling his frustration.

When canvassing the neighbors didn't get them anywhere, Ray and Glenn began interviewing people directly connected to both Debbie and *Style Weekly*.

"What you do is you do a history on her," Ray says. "You gotta find out who the victim is in any homicide case. So when you start doing background on her or him, [you] see what kind of lifestyle they led, see what kind of habits they had, persons they hung out with and everything."

Through his interviews with family, coworkers and neighbors, Ray Williams rapidly pieced together a picture of Debbie Davis' life. And those pieces didn't add up to homicide, especially one this heinous and cruel. Debbie led a quiet life. She wasn't dating anyone. She hadn't talked to her ex-husband in years. She didn't use drugs. She didn't hang out in bars. She wasn't a prostitute. She tended to dress plainly and was a little on the plump side. As best as Ray could tell, she was a kind, bookish woman who liked to bake cookies and lived a modest, maybe somewhat lonely life in an apartment with her two cats.

So then Ray theorized that perhaps the murder had been motivated by someone who was angry at *Style*. Maybe it was someone who didn't like something *Style* wrote. Maybe it was an obsessed reader. Or maybe it was someone who owed *Style* money. Either way, Ray began thinking that it was possible that perhaps the killing had been a case of mistaken identity and the intended target had actually been *Style*'s publisher, Lorna Wyckoff.

Style Weekly **magazine founder Lorna Wyckoff** (*Photo by Scott Elmquist*)

"We had police around our home," recounts Wyckoff. "It was a very frightening time, to have someone knock on the door and tell you that someone you know has been murdered and that it could have possibly been meant for you. It was a pretty alarming situation."

Wyckoff had just lost her dear friend George Stoddard, the former press secretary to U.S. Senator Charles Robb, to cancer earlier that year. Now Debbie Davis had been murdered. "And then a few months later," Wyckoff says, "my husband's parents were both killed in a car accident, which was pretty tragic. For me personally, it was a really hard year. And that part with Debbie was as horrific as anything that you could imagine — probably the worst thing that ever happened in my life, I would say, because it was so brutal and violent and I was right in the middle of it all."

In the weeks following Debbie's murder, the Williams Boys would come by Wyckoff's house late at night and talk over their theories. Sometimes they'd show Wyckoff the crime scene photos.

"I saw a lot of things that I wish I'd never seen and continue to this day to be a nightmare for me. ... It got darker and deeper and more upsetting," Wyckoff recalls. The state medical examiner's office, she was told, had determined that Davis, the sweet lady who doted on her pet cats and kept candy on her desk and enjoyed decorating the office for holidays, had been raped and tortured to death for hours. The way she was tied up, the more Debbie struggled, the more her bonds tightened. The killer had relaxed his literal stranglehold on the poor woman again and again, bringing her to the brink of death and letting up, until she finally expired in fear, pain and exhaustion.

"She regained consciousness again and then he would start to strangle her again, so that there was some degree of torture," Wyckoff says, "like she was an animal, a young bird or a little thing that he was watching die. He enjoyed watching her die."

It wasn't immediately clear to investigators that Debbie had been raped or sexually assaulted.

"Some serial killers are exhibitionists" and leave their victims posed in sexually explicit or humiliating ways as part of their ritual of killing, Williams says, "but he clothed her, put her shorts back on.

It indicates psychologically that he was ashamed of what he did and didn't want her to be found."

After Debbie Davis's murder, police had spent 72 hours combing Debbie Davis' house and came up empty on fingerprints. The only thing they knew the killer left behind were large semen stains on the curtains, bed linens and Davis' body, apparently from masturbating during the crime.

The forensics technicians who searched the apartment came up with an unidentified Caucasian hair and one hair that may have come from a person of African descent. But there are lots of ways stray hairs can make it into a crime scene. It didn't mean that any of them came from the killer.

As for why the killer had abandoned Debbie's car barely two blocks from her apartment, Williams observes, "That's a main thoroughfare for the cops to [patrol.] So I guarantee you he got nervous because he couldn't shift the gears and he got out and walked the rest of the way."

Meanwhile, at *Style Weekly*, Debbie Davis' friends and coworkers were shell-shocked, struggling with their grief and fear. Publisher Lorna Wyckoff offered a $10,000 reward for information leading to the capture and conviction of Debbie's killer.

The weekend of the murder, Wyckoff called all of the magazine's employees and assembled them at her home for an impromptu wake led by well-known local Episcopal priest the Rev. Ben Campbell, who would later conduct a Richmond-area memorial service for Debbie at St. Paul's Episcopal Church downtown. Campbell asked Debbie's coworkers to write notes with their favorite memories of her and share them aloud with each other.

"Over the course of the weekend," Wyckoff recalls, "we slowly gathered our friends together and all of our colleagues and clients and everybody who had known Debbie and just spent the weekend in tears holding each other crying, sad and devastated. ... It was just a real moment of remorse and crying and mourning for our friend."

About a week and a half after the murder, Wyckoff traveled to Debbie's home city of Lynchburg for the funeral, where she was shocked to learn that it was an open-casket service, which is often traditional in Southern states. Seated five feet away, she couldn't bring herself to look at her murdered friend's corpse.

As Wyckoff sat and opened the funeral program, she was further surprised to discover that she was listed as the eulogist. Lost in their anguish, Debbie's parents had apparently forgotten to ask her to speak.

"I found that out about five minutes before the service was to start," Wyckoff says, "and I thought, 'OK, I can do this. I can rise to this occasion.' Having been a teacher, I really thankfully wasn't afraid of speaking in front of people. But there was a moment, about three or four minutes of sheer panic, until I realized I had these letters."

Wyckoff had brought the notes containing her employees' memories of Debbie, intending to give them to the Dudleys. "And so I thought, this is perfect. I can talk about these letters." Debbie wasn't just *her* friend, *Style's* publisher told the gathered congregation; she was *everybody's* friend.

Debbie's cousin Judy played the organ at the funeral, which was held on their grandmother's 98th birthday. "It was a Lynchburg funeral," she says, laughing. "Much more religious than Debbie would have wanted."

Among the mourners, Ray and Glenn Williams kept a watchful eye for anyone suspicious. Police surreptitiously filmed and photographed the funerals of all the South Side Strangler's victims in hopes that a suspect might emerge. They did the same thing outside the crime scenes.

Investigative reporter Lisa Antonelli Bacon started working as a staff writer at *Style* just after the murder. She would later report on the killings.

Debbie Davis "had been killed like two weeks before I came to *Style*. It was really odd to come to this place," Bacon recalls. "Everybody is very close and I was the outsider. It was like, it was really strange. People were walking around like zombies because it was a brutal murder of someone that they'd spent every day with."

"Everybody had their own sense of tragedy or sadness," Wyckoff says. "It was very, very hard, very hard. And then it turned into panic because this guy was roaming around murdering people."

"It was horrible and scary and sad," remembers author Frances Schultz. The former host of the award-winning cable TV show *Southern Living Presents*, Schultz worked as an editor at *Style* at the time of the murder. "Debbie was beloved by all and not anyone you could ever imagine had enemies, let alone someone who wanted her dead, which left some of us thinking it was just some sick deranged wretch who could have done it before and who might have done it again."

Deona Houff remembers everyone at the magazine being sorrowful and frightened in the aftermath – and hoping the murderer wasn't someone they knew or, god forbid, worked with.

"We didn't know it was a serial killer," Houff says. "I assumed it was somebody who knew Debbie. It was a very scary time."

Former *Style* art director Kent Eanes says he never felt like he or anyone who else worked with Debbie at the magazine were ever considered suspects in the murder, even after he volunteered the information to detectives that he had been at Debbie's apartment just a few nights prior to the murder when she had called and asked him to take her to the emergency room.

Instead, Eanes says, the questions that the Williams Boys asked "were more like, 'Did you know any of Debbie's friends outside of work? Did you know if she had any enemies?' But no one ever asked, 'Where were you on the night of the murder?'"

A week or so prior to the slaying, Eanes had been taking photos for a cover issue about people with unusual pets and he introduced Debbie, who was an animal lover, to one of the men who had come in for the photo shoot. "I brought him downstairs and introduced him to Debbie and they kind of hit it off and chatted and she enjoyed [his] pet. And at some point that individual became a person of interest but only for a short period of time," he says.

Within two weeks of the murder to the day, it would become apparent to the police and everyone else that Debbie's killing had nothing to do with *Style* after the South Side Strangler struck again.

"Once there was another murder," Houff says, "I started realizing it was something else bad going on in the city. It had to do with her neighborhood, not where she worked."

Thirty years later, Judy Fiske and her husband Eric still live in the same house, a block and a half away from where her cousin Debbie Davis was murdered.

"There's a sadness that goes with you all the time," Judy says. "Because she lived so close to us, you know, [we] ride by the house all the time. I often wonder who lives in that apartment and how they live there. It's like, I don't want to tell you what went on there. But somebody lives in it."

CHAPTER 2

POWDER KEG

It was a little before 1:45 a.m. on Saturday, October 3, 1987, when Marcel Slag pulled up to the spacious, old two-story Colonial home he shared with his wife, Dr. Susan Hellams, in Richmond's tranquil Woodland Heights neighborhood, cater-corner from Woodland Heights Baptist Church.

As a fifth-year senior neurosurgery resident at Virginia Commonwealth University's Medical College of Virginia, it wasn't uncommon for Susan to work late hours but she had told Marcel she'd there when he got home that night.

Then a law student at George Washington University in Washington, D.C., Marcel lived in Silver Spring, Maryland, on the weekdays. He commuted south to Richmond on the weekends to be with his wife at their home on 31st Street, a few blocks away from Forest Hill Park and the James River.

As Marcel opened the door, he thought he could hear Susan moving around upstairs. Maybe he woke her? Mindful that she needed her sleep, he took a quick shower before silently creeping into their dark bedroom, lit only by the faint yellow-ish orange glow of the sodium street lights down the block.

Something was wrong.

He turned the bedroom light on and saw crimson spots on the unmade bed.

Blood.

Instantaneously, his eyes landed on a sight straight out of a horror movie: Susan's nude, dead body was sprawled half out of their bi-fold closet on the wooden floorboards. A red leather woman's belt was tied tightly around her neck. Another belt, this one black, was tethered to it like a dog leash. The killer had yanked it back to strangle her.

Her head was shoved between the closet wall and a small white suitcase. Lying on her stomach, her long black skirt and slip were hiked up above her waist. The murderer had tied a quilted magenta belt around her left ankle. Bent at the knees, her lower legs and feet were stuck awkwardly in the air. She was wearing her thick, red, crew-knit wool socks and one matching red shoe. Her hands were bound firmly behind her back with an extension cord and a navy blue woman's necktie.

Her fractured nose and bruised mouth were caked in fresh blood. Her skin was still warm. Her wide-open eyes were dotted red.

A slight breeze entered in through the open bedroom window.

Born in Charleston, South Carolina, in 1955, Susan Elizabeth Hellams grew up in the middle-class Richmond, Virginia, suburbs of Henrico County. Her father was a chemist and her mother was an elementary school teacher who passed down her love of reading and learning to her only daughter.

After graduating Tucker High School, Susan attended the prestigious University of Virginia, which was founded by Thomas Jefferson, in Charlottesville, Virginia. She would later receive her undergraduate degree from the University of Richmond before enrolling in medical school at Virginia Commonwealth University's Medical College of Virginia, better known around Richmond as MCV.

Her mentor and supervisor was Dr. Harold Young, a talented neurosurgeon who'd served as a combat surgeon in the Vietnam War.

"It took us all a long time to heal. And you know wounds heal but memories last forever. I'll never forget her," says Young, who's still a practicing doctor at VCU Health System, where the university's neurosurgical center is named for him. A conference room at the center is named after Hellams. A plaque outside the hallway bears her photo: a long-haired young redhead with pale skin, kind eyes and a toothy smile.

Dr. Susan Hellams was the first female neurosurgery resident accepted into the Medical College of Virginia's demanding program.

"I have three daughters. She was like a fourth daughter," Young says. "My wife and I were really were very fond of her because she was just such a neat person. … Everybody was shocked. And I think it took a long time to recover from that."

Young recalls his young protégé as "a very special lady. In my mind, she had all … the attributes of being a surgeon. There's sort of a saying in surgery: What makes a great surgeon? The answer is a person who has the eyes of an eagle, the heart of a lion and the hands of a woman. And she had it all. I thought she would have been a great surgeon. And she was such a compassionate caregiver. She really loved people and she had a passion for what she did.

"She had class, character, grace and elegance and she usually wore long beautiful skirts and would often walk around the hospital late in the evening seeing the poor patients, the patients who weren't getting maybe all the necessary attention because they weren't private patients … but she would always make certain they got excellent care."

During her time at MCV, Susan Hellams divorced her first husband, a fellow medical student at MCV. In the messy aftermath of the divorce, she moved to France from 1983 through 1984, where she served as the chief resident at the American Hospital of Paris before she decided to return to the neurosurgery program at MCV. While in France, she fell in love with Dutch lawyer Marcel Slag and the two swiftly married. Paris was her favorite place on Earth, she told friends.

One of her fellow residents at the time, Dr. John Nestler, is now the chair of VCU's Department of Internal Medicine. Close friends with Susan, Nestler frequently socialized with her and Marcel and they would dine at each other's homes.

Susan Hellams, he says, "was a true renaissance lady. That term gets tossed around a lot, but she truly was one. She was foremost a scientist. That's why she went into neurosurgery. She loved medicine. She loved science. At the same time, however, she loved the arts: classical music, any opera, anything, she was enthralled with it. She was [also] a voracious reader."

"She was a very nice person, super conscientious, a super-good doctor [with] great bedside manner [and was] very, very concerned about her patients," says Dr. Lynn Atkinson, a retired neurosurgeon in Florida who started her neurosurgery residency a year behind Hellams at MCV. "She was very hardworking, very dedicated and [had a] wonderful, glowing personality, a great smile – very, very friendly."

As a senior neurosurgery resident, Hellams had about 20 more months to go in her residency before she'd be a practicing, independent neurosurgeon. Medical residents work notoriously long hours and she was no exception, sometimes putting in as many as 100 hours per week at the hospital.

"Neurosurgery is a very tough residency," Young says. "It is very demanding and in the '70s and '80s we did not have a lot of women who wanted to go into neurosurgery. It was a very challenging residency."

In fact, Hellams had been the first woman to enter the neurosurgery program at MCV.

Neurosurgeon Dr. Harold Young was Hellams' mentor at Virginia Commonwealth University's Medical College of Virginia. "She was like a ... daughter," he says.

"Dr. Hellams was a female in neurosurgery during a time when you did not see [many] females entering that field," says Dr. Colleen Kraft, who was a pediatrics resident at MCV during the time that Hellams was a neurosurgery resident.

"Dr. Hellams was extremely dedicated. The neurosurgeons work very long hours and at the time the neurosurgical residents worked harder than I think almost any other residents. But she was, she was always pleasant, she was always very complete and always very dedicated to her patients," Kraft recalls.

Now the high-profile president of the American Academy of Pediatrics, Kraft was a familiar face on CNN and MSNBC in summer 2018 as a leading, vocal critic of the Trump Administration's policy of detaining young undocumented immigrant children and separating them from their parents.

She was also among a handful of people who were the last to see Susan Hellams alive.

"Thirty years ago [Dr. Susan Hellams] was quite a force to be reckoned with because she was intelligent, she was responsive [and] she was communicative," Kraft says. "If she was on call, you were always glad because she would answer your questions. She would come to see your patients [and] she would be very complete in her assessment and a great communicator with both the pediatrician on call and the family."

On Friday, October 2, 1987, Hellams had assisted on a spinal neck surgery with Young – their last operation of the day. Around 6:30 p.m., they parted ways.

"We'd made rounds and we walked down the hallway together to the elevator to the North Hospital," Young says. "I can remember to this day she's wearing a brown skirt down to her ankles and I was going down the elevator and she was going into the ward to see a patient in the North Hospital and we said, 'So long, see you next Monday' or whenever. I don't think I was going to see her that weekend."

The patient she was headed to see that evening was under Kraft's care at the Children's Hospital, where Hellams was often called to assist in caring for children with brain cancers or injuries necessitating cerebral shunts.

"We had admitted a young child with a brain tumor," remembers Kraft, "so Dr. Hellams came and consulted with us on this child and she and I were talking, it was a Friday night. We were both looking forward to going home and we decided to walk out to the parking garage together [afterwards]. At the time Virginia Commonwealth University was not a particularly safe place to be around. And you always wanted to walk out to the parking garage with another person as a single female. We said goodbye and have a nice weekend and went our separate ways."

After that, Susan stopped at her house and left a note for her husband in case he arrived home early. Then she drove to the House of Hunan Gourmet Chinese restaurant on West Broad Street in Richmond to meet friends for dinner: Dr. Nuala Sinisi, her husband, Jeffrey Wright, and MCV neurosurgery resident Dr. Lynn Atkinson.

Sinisi, an anesthesiologist and former MCV resident who was good friends with Hellams, was in town with her husband, Jeffrey Wright. They had traveled from Texas so Sinisi could interview for a job opening at MCV.

"It was just a regular dinner, you know? We went and got Chinese food and caught up on what everybody was doing," Atkinson recalls.

At around 10 p.m., they all left the restaurant and Susan accompanied Sinisi and Wright back to their hotel, spending the next 45 minutes chatting with them before she said she needed to head home to bed. Jeffrey Wright offered to follow her to make sure she got home OK, but Susan declined, telling him that it wasn't necessary because she lived in a safe neighborhood.

Hellams had Saturday off so the Wrights made plans to meet Susan and Marcel the next morning for a day trip to the mountains about two hours west of Richmond.

That would never happen.

"My phone rang at probably 4 or 5 in the morning," Young recalls sadly. It was the police. They "told me that [Susan] had been murdered, brutally murdered. It was a horrible, horrible, horrible, situation as they described it to me. And I remember just sitting there stunned."

The call rousted Richmond Police Detective Ray Williams out of bed at 2:20 a.m. Like all homicide detectives, Ray knew that sleep was only a luxury. You can sleep when you're dead.

Ray made it to the scene just ahead of his partner, Glenn Williams.

"When Glenn got there, I said, 'The same son of a bitch killed Debbie Davis killed her.' I said, 'We in trouble. He knows what he's doing.'"

The victim's distraught husband had called in the murder, relaying the horrific details in his thick Dutch accent through tears. "Hello? My wife … my wife has been murdered," Marcel Slag had told the emergency 911 dispatcher in a call at 1:56 a.m.

"You know who murdered her?" the dispatcher asked.

"No, I am living in Washington. I … I come home, there is blood and she is lying in the closet. Oh please come, please!" he implored.

Nearly an hour later, the guy was still a wreck. Ray could tell that Slag clearly wasn't his wife's killer. "We ruled him out pretty quickly," he says.

The house was lit by flashing red and blue police-car lights. "There were so many police vehicles, we could barely get down the block," recalls former EMT Gary York, who was in the ambulance crew that responded to the call to transport a body to the morgue. "Just the amount of police presence there was pretty astounding. They weren't sharing a lot of information with us at all. It was very unusual. It was not the normal DOA, that's for sure."

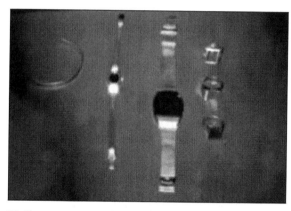

Hellams removed her jewelry, placing it on the fireplace mantel in her bedroom shortly before she was attacked.

Hellams' home was a little under a mile east from where *Style Weekly* magazine accounts manager Debbie Davis had been strangled exactly two weeks prior, just on the other side of Forest Hill Park.

Inside, up in the second-floor master bedroom, Ray and Glenn found Susan Hellams' nude body, where it still lay, unceremoniously crammed into the closet. Her body was on the floorboards, with her legs and buttocks protruding out the closet door.

Nearby, a small bookcase was filled with anatomy books and other medical tomes. The latest issue of Vogue magazine, with supermodel Cindy Crawford on the cover wearing a low-cut red dress and sporting emerald earrings, lay on Susan's nightstand. She had carefully placed her watch and bracelet on the mantelpiece in her bedroom as she prepared for bed. The Strangler, Ray Williams says, "was apparently hiding in the closet, watching her do all that."

Two facts were immediately apparent to the Williams Boys: One, the killing was sexually motivated. And, two, it was clearly the work of the first known serial killer in modern Richmond memory.

After the Davis murder "we were concerned," Ray Williams says, "but after Susan Hellams' [murder], we knew we were dealing with somebody awfully dangerous and awfully smart."

Amazingly, just weeks before, Ray had completed a 10-month course of study about serial killers with the Federal Bureau of Investigations' elite Behavioral Science Unit at the FBI Training Academy in Quantico, Virginia, located about an hour-and-a-half's drive north of Richmond. Ray had been one of 50 homicide detectives selected from across the nation to learn about a still-new investigative method called behavioral profiling.

Immortalized in the Oscar-winning film *The Silence of the Lambs* and the Netflix series *Mindhunter*, the FBI Behavioral Science unit is where pioneering FBI agents Robert Ressler and John Douglas first coined the phrase "serial killer" and developed our modern understanding of how these real-life monsters operate.

In the mid-1970s, a little more than a decade before the South Side Strangler killings, Ressler and Douglas theorized that they could identify suspects in serial killings based upon common traits, as well as the offenders' modus operandi and the evidence they left behind at crime scenes. Their research led them to prisons across America, where they conducted in-depth, taped interviews with some of the most infamous serial killers of the 20th century, including Ted Bundy, John Wayne Gacy, Edmund Kemper and Jeffrey Dahmer.

For Ray, the fact that he had just finished studying about serial killers and then stumbled right into the only known serial killing in Richmond history was too coincidental to be a coincidence, as the famed New York Yankees and New York Mets manager Yogi Berra once said.

"Somebody wanted me to have both of those cases," Ray Williams says in his raspy Southern drawl, his belief in a higher power firmly evident.

Unlike the Davis murder scene, this time a couple items were determined to be missing from the home: Susan Hellams' violin and her diamond ring. The Williams Boys had no idea whether the killer had taken the valuables to sell or to keep as trophies.

As for how the murderer had gained entrance into the house in the first place, that was anything but a mystery, thanks to the open window. He had clearly climbed onto the six-foot-tall backyard fence, hoisted himself up onto the back porch roof and then climbed onto the tarpaper-covered back balcony, which had a couple chairs and a broken-down air conditioning unit on it. The balcony was right beside the master bedroom window.

More confirmation that the guy was athletic and agile, probably young and muscular, Ray thought: "We knew he had to [have] a strong build to pull himself up onto that damn porch."

The South Side Strangler scaled a six-foot wooden fence (*left*) and hoisted himself onto the second-story porch roof to gain entrance into Dr. Susan Hellams' bedroom window. He left behind a jar of Vaseline on the balcony (*upper right*).

Ray would later learn that Susan Hellams made a habit of keeping her window open so her cat could get in and out. This time, she had left the screen down. No matter; the South Side Strangler had neatly sliced it out. And he had most likely been hiding in her bedroom closet when Susan returned home that night from having dinner and visiting with her friends.

One of the killer's shoes had left a smudge of roofing tar from the tarpapered balcony on the bedroom floor. There was another tar smudge on Susan's right calf, where the Strangler had stomped his foot down, bracing against her leg for leverage while he pulled on the belts to choke her. He also left large amounts of semen on Susan's slip and skirt, evidently from masturbating. The only other trace of the killer in the bedroom were the impression of his knees that he left on a cushion resting on the window seat as he exited.

"He apparently was putting her in the closet as the front door opened because he threw stuff out of the way and Marcel said that he heard somebody upstairs [but] it couldn't have been Susan. She's already dead," Ray Williams says. "So [the killer] went back out the same window."

Outside, sitting on the old air conditioning unit on the balcony was an open jar of Vaseline that the Strangler had set down and forgotten in his haste. (He had used the Vaseline as lubricant in the rape. Some of Susan Hellams' pubic hairs were found inside the jar and Vaseline was found on her body.) The murderer also dropped a three-foot length of white rope, which had landed in a large clay flowerpot below. No question about it: The Strangler had definitely been in a hurry to leave.

Investigators would later trace the lot number off the Vaseline jar to a drugstore at Beaufont Plaza, a strip shopping center across Midlothian Turnpike from nearby Cloverleaf Mall, where victim Debbie Davis had worked a couple nights a week at the Waldenbooks store.

Medical examiners would determine that Susan Hellams had been raped vaginally and rectally, just like Davis. Davis had also suffered bruising and tearing to her vaginal tissue.

Dr. Marcella Fierro, one of the top forensic pathologists in the nation, performed autopsies on some the South Side Strangler's victims. Now retired from her job as chief medical examiner for the commonwealth of Virginia, Fierro is a legend around Richmond, where she's known as a both a stellar court witness and a passionate advocate for the dead.

"They were my patients – the only thing I didn't do that other doctors do is I didn't listen to their chests," Fierro says. "I took [a medical] history, I did a physical examination, requested laboratory studies, made diagnoses. I do what doctors do. ... They deserve their dignity in death. It was my job to make sure they had it."

Over the span of her 40-plus-year career, Fierro saw death and suffering in myriad forms but these murders stand out in her memory. They bothered her. They were violations of the basic sanctity of home and hearth: "It was awfully cruel," she says. "Her home was invaded and she was killed in her own place and very cruelly strangled."

When she performed the autopsy, Fierro noted smelling a "faint musky odor" on Susan Hellams' body. So Fierro utilized a then-new procedure, scanning the body for evidence with a laser. It was so sensitive that it could have detected fingerprints on the body (had there been any). The laser revealed the presence of semen on Hellams' breasts, buttocks and vaginal region.

"I was very finicky about that. I didn't make any assumptions that sexual assault did not occur. We know that half of women who are sexually assaulted don't show any injury," Fierro points out.

"Women who are sexually active may not show much injury, if any. And so it's not something that appears foremost in some people's minds. But being a woman, and recognizing that information from the literature that you could certainly have sexual assault without injury, I think made me more cognizant of the fact that it could occur and so I would check, I would test for it more often."

❖

In the wake of Hellams' murder, Ray and Glenn Williams worked for three sleepless days and nights, canvassing the neighborhood, chasing down any leads they could find. "We went home long enough to take a shower, change suits and come back. We stayed up 72 straight hours," Ray Williams remembers.

The merciless and seemingly random murders of innocent people attract lots of unwanted heat and attention from the community, elected officials, the police brass – and especially the news media.

Within two days of the second slaying, the local press had bestowed a nickname on the murderer: the South Side Strangler. (It's unclear who coined the name; it didn't come from police. It may have been the invention of TV news reporters. The city newspapers only used the phrase twice during fall 1987, first referencing the "so-called South Side Strangler," an acknowledgment that the moniker was in already in use.)

And with the realization that there was a serial killer at large in the city, Richmond erupted into fear. Hardware stores sold out of deadbolts. People locked their doors and nailed their windows shut. Women slept over at friends' houses rather than stay home alone.

"The impact was indescribable," remembers Kraft. "People were paralyzed with fear. People would travel at least in twos. People were afraid to drive home alone or go into a home alone. It was really very disruptive. People who lived alone often wouldn't stay alone in their apartment. They would stay with a friend and then that friend would stay with them on alternate nights because we were just so scared. If something this awful could happen to a person with the intellect and the responsibility of Dr. Hellams, [we realized] it could happen to any of us."

"It just terrorized the city," recalls former *Style Weekly* magazine creative director Kent Eanes. "It just spooked everyone. In fact, I remember I lived at home at the time. It was prior to my being married and I got so scared to the point that I would start taking baths instead of showers – because I could hear if someone was coming into the house, or at least I thought I could. That's the point of paranoia that I reached."

In the South Side neighborhoods of Forest Hill, Westover Hills and Woodland Heights, hundreds of folks gathered at community meetings shortly after Hellams' murder, demanding answers and action from police and politicians.

A local state delegate, two city council members, the city manager, the city prosecutor and police officials all showed up for a meeting at Woodland Heights Baptist Church, diagonally across the street from where Susan Hellams had died in terror less than a week before.

"I'm frightened for my family. I'm afraid for myself. But we must turn it into something that's going to help us," City Councilman Drew Gillespie said, calling for neighbors to band together.

"There is not a higher priority in city government, from the city administration's standpoint, than bringing this person or persons who have committed these homicides to trial," Richmond City Manager Robert C. Bobb assured the gathered neighbors, asking them not to panic. (Strangely, this was the second city helmed by Bobb that had been plunged into fear by a serial killer. Before taking his job in Richmond, Bobb had served as city manager of Santa Ana, California, during the 1985 spate of area home-invasion rapes and murders committed by Richard Ramirez, the notorious Night Stalker serial killer.)

Police urged South Side residents to report anything out of the ordinary – such as out-of-place vehicles or strangers in the neighborhood. And with just weeks to go before Halloween, the Woodland Heights neighborhood association discussed whether to cancel trick or treating or limit it to daylight hours.

"The police message at this community meeting in Forest Hills is security: Lock up your house, keep the outside lights on, keep an eye on strangers," a WRVA 1140 AM reporter said in a news broadcast from the scene.

Angry and afraid, neighbors weren't entirely thrilled with what the police and city government officials were telling them. Residents wanted more police on the streets and they wanted the police doing more to catch the killer before he could strike again.

"I think we all were hoping to hear something actually about what's been going on, to learn some more information about it, more so than to be told to lock your windows," one neighbor told WRVA.

Sadly, 19 years later, the Woodland Heights neighborhood would again be the site of one of the most gruesome chapters in Richmond history when Bryan and Kathryn Harvey and their two daughters, Stella, 9, and Ruby, 4, were viciously slain in a home-invasion robbery by spree killers Ricky Javon Gray and Ray Dandridge. The Harvey family was also murdered on 31st Street, just four blocks up the street north from where Susan Hellams was killed.

Ray and Glenn Williams didn't need to be told to work harder on the Davis and Hellams murder cases. They were running down every angle they could. They chased down local sex offenders, grilled prison inmates and interviewed the victims' friends and co-workers – all with fruitless results. Ray also looked for commonalities between the two victims – did they know each other? Debbie Davis had a surgery performed at MCV – could that be the connection?

"For the first six weeks, it was very frustrating," remembers Ray. "For six weeks, we were spinning our wheels. We were [canvassing] door to door down on Forest Hill Avenue just to see if we got lucky. You're looking for suspects [and] we'd reach a point where [a suspect] would look good – and boom! [We'd] hit a dead end."

The Williams Boys interviewed one guy who had an honest-to-god sex dungeon in his basement. Turns out he was just an S&M aficionado. While patrolling the Forest Hill neighborhood looking for the killer, Ray pulled over a car full of four undercover narcotics officers who were out hunting for drug dealers. He was furious.

"I got a suspicious vehicle call – we ended up stopping them and we recognized them as soon as we stopped them."

"Y'all are out patrolling around here at night with no headlights on! The damn public's scared enough! Y'all need to find somewhere else to work!" Ray scolded.

"We shooed them away from Forest Hill. We didn't need the added aggravation."

And then there was the MCV orderly who confessed to murdering Dr. Susan Hellams.

"Well, he said he did it," says Ray, "so I said, 'Tell me how you did it.' 'Well, I beat her first and...' We knew five seconds after talking with him [that] he didn't do it. I said, 'Man, you crazy, inventing something you didn't do!' He was looking for 15 minutes of fame. So we eliminated him quickly. He was a little strange [so] I notified MCV and VCU [to] keep an eye on this guy."

Before long, Ray says, he and Glenn had interviewed "over 400 damn people and still hadn't developed any suspects so, yeah, it was tedious and we worked all hours of the day and night."

The Williams boys did, however, uncover one promising piece of evidence: Wading through financial records at the Cloverleaf Mall Waldenbooks store where Debbie Davis worked part-time, Ray found a check written by Hellams. It was endorsed on the back by Debbie Davis.

"It just gives you cold chills," recalls Williams. "In all my experience I didn't think anything would surprise me in a homicide investigation, but this thing knocked me off my feet."

Meanwhile, FBI agents had worked up a profile of the Strangler – in their opinion, he was probably white, very intelligent and either lived alone or with a domineering female figure. He was someone who was extremely combative towards women and had difficulty dating or holding a job, they theorized. It's possible that he could have a criminal record. He committed the murders on Friday nights, they thought, because he probably worked weekdays and didn't want to see anyone after he killed. It was likely that he had been stalking the women and was stealing items from the murder scenes to keep as trophies.

With public pressure mounting, the Richmond Police Department formed a task force dedicated to catching the Strangler. They pulled every available detective along with the investigative Street Crimes Unit and also detailed the entire SNAP squad to the case.

SNAP, or Selected Neighborhood Action Patrol, was an elite group of patrolmen who provided law enforcement during the early morning hours in high-crime areas. Now they were patrolling Forest Hill and Woodland Heights, watching for burglars and shadowing suspects, as well as seeking out any single women who they thought might make attractive targets for the Strangler. They wound up placing 12 women under surveillance who fit the investigators' profile of likely next targets for the Strangler, completely unbeknownst to the women themselves.

"Anything that moved got stopped," Ray Williams says. "We'd walk the neighborhoods and hide and hopefully we'd see [the Strangler] patrolling. We had the task force units lying in bushes. They would get into strategic locations and lay there all night long to see if they saw any movement."

This reallocation of resources angered residents in the high-crime areas that suddenly found themselves without police patrols, however.

Sa'ad El-Amin, a controversial, firebrand attorney and civic activist who would later serve on City Council before being sent to federal prison on tax fraud charges, was outraged that the city police had pulled the SNAP team out of poor, majority black neighborhoods that were beginning to see body counts rising from the burgeoning 1980s crack cocaine epidemic.

"It's a powder keg out there," El-Amin told WRVA at the time. "A lot of black people are angry at this disproportionate response. They feel that black life and black property is valueless compared to white life and white property, which appears to be more valuable."

Just as the James River's rapids bisect Richmond, the former capital of the Confederate States of America is also deeply divided by its long and ugly racial history, steeped in slavery and segregation.

Confederate flags were proudly and openly displayed just about everywhere in the Richmond region throughout the 20th century and some area schools still bear the names of Confederate leaders to this day. Twenty-century textbooks in the South often sanitized and glossed over slavery, the ultimate Southern nightmare and America's Original Sin, in some cases making the sale of human beings sound as benign as the trade of corn or tobacco. As late as 1968, Richmond's newspapers still divided real estate listings into ads for black and white homes. Local schools didn't really begin desegregating until the early 1970s.

As crack cocaine started hitting the city in the '80s, it became all too commonplace for young black men to be gunned down in the streets, a byproduct of the drug trade and its associated turf wars. Within a few years of the South Side Strangler murders, Richmond would be called the Murder Capital of the South. Murders steadily escalated from 50 or 60 a year in the early 1980s to a high of 140 by 1997. Innocent bystanders would sometimes get caught in the crossfire of the gang violence. People in the city's majority African-American neighborhoods were in turmoil.

And the last thing overwhelmed police and prosecutors needed was the South Side Strangler, says Assistant Commonwealth's Attorney Learned Barry: "You got this crazy guy going around. You've got a serial killer on the loose. And we're going from 50 murders a year into the hundreds. So not only do we have a nutcase running loose, we've got the murder rate skyrocketing. So it was like a double whammy."

All of the homicides and drug cases left understaffed and beleaguered police and prosecutors struggling to keep up.

"When you have a killing every two or three days, you start to lose track of things" but then the Strangler cases happened and everything changed because of "the brutality of it," Barry says, and the fact that these were "not people that are involved in the drug business. I mean, these are good people being killed in an *awful* way.

"There are certain places that in the city of Richmond where, if you're involved in the drug trade, you probably got a good shot at getting hurt or killed. But [with] *these* [killings], you were like, how did *this* happen? You know, who in the world would hurt *these* people?"

❖

As the police investigation into Susan Hellams' murder continued, her shell-shocked loved ones and co-workers were left to grieve while the city remained under a shadow of fear.

"People were so upset," Kraft says. "I remember going and seeing some of the staff at the medical school and they were just crying and in tears and couldn't believe it."

"We all still miss her. I still think about her," Nestler says, sorrowfully.

Susan wasn't interested in going into private practice when she finished her residency, he recalls: "She wanted to go into academic medicine and become a researcher in the area of neurosurgery. And I'm sure she would have excelled in that role and she would have made major contributions."

Looking back on that terrifying and distressing time, Nestler says, "We were all devastated when she died. And who would have thought that something like *that* could happen in Richmond?"

CHAPTER 3

ESCALATION

Someone was stalking Diane Cho.

The 15-year-old Manchester High School freshman had confided in her best friend, Jenny Han, about a disturbing, recurring nightmare she'd been having.

"She was suffering, having dreams about someone following her and stuff," remembers Jenny, who lived upstairs from Diane in the low-income Chesterfield Village apartment complex, just across the busy, eight-lane Midlothian Turnpike from Cloverleaf Mall in suburban Chesterfield County. The dreams, Diane told Jenny, would end with a crucifix flying closer and closer towards Diane's forehead.

Jenny wasn't the only person to whom Diane confessed these fears. She also talked about it with her friend and classmate Desiree Fierros, who goes by Desi, and who lived in the same South Side apartment complex as Diane and Jenny, right near the border of Chesterfield and Richmond.

"For about two weeks, she kept telling us that she had seen this man following her and that she had gone to the mall and seen him," Desi recalls. "She just told us that she thought somebody was following her. So for about two weeks, she kept telling us that she had seen this man following her and that she had gone to the mall and she saw him. She saw him when she was waiting for the school bus."

Nevertheless, Diane refused to seek help from her parents or other adults about the problem.

"She made us promise never to tell anybody, not to tell my mom, her parents, anybody, about this guy because she had said that her parents were very strict Korean and wouldn't let her go out often," Desi says. "So, like, when she was allowed out, she had a strict curfew. Her parents always knew where she was. They didn't really like the idea of her going out. So she was afraid that, like, if they ever thought that somebody was following her, they wouldn't let her go out anymore."

One night in mid-November 1987, Diane was at Cloverleaf Mall's newly built nine-screen multiplex cinema with Desi and another friend, buying tickets to see the movie *The Princess Bride*, when Diane began trembling with fright and pointed out her stalker, who was staring at both girls from across the parking lot.

"I'll never forget," says Desi. "I'm looking at Diane. She was pale to begin with – she never went out into the sun or anything – but she just got, like, completely sheet-white and I'll never forget the look on her face: [It] was like a look of sheer fright that I have never to this day seen before. She was so pale. So I was asking her what was happening ... you know, what was the matter? I wasn't sure. She couldn't talk. She just pointed. And I remember I looked and I saw this man. He was in the parking lot, standing next to a car.

"To this day, I can close my eyes and see that animal standing there looking at me. His eyes were hollow. It wasn't normal," Desi says. "It was the coldest look I've ever seen in my life."

Diane Cho and her family had immigrated to the United States from South Korea just three years prior, in 1984, and it had barely been five months since they moved to Richmond.

Her father, Jong Chul Cho, was a draftsman from Seoul. He and Diane's mother, Hyun Kyoung Cho, had first lived with Diane and her younger brother Robert at an apartment complex in Maryland, where Jong's brother and mother lived. However, due to Jong's poor command of English, he couldn't find a job in his field, so he began working at a grocery store. Diane's mother took a job in a deli.

Diane Cho's father, Jong Chul Cho, and mother, Hyun Kyoung Cho, moved their family to the United States in 1984. (*Photo courtesy Cho family***)**

At the time the Cho family arrived in America, Diane was 12 and Robert was 9. Their uncle had given them their new American names. The whole thing felt pretty arbitrary to Robert, who these days calls himself Roman, a nickname he picked up in high school.

"My name was ... my name *is* Sung Won, my Korean name. And my sister's name was Jung Won," says Roman Cho, now a Los-Angeles-based portrait photographer whose work has appeared in *TIME*, *GQ* and *Rolling Stone* magazines. "For a while, it was just her and I. And we didn't really know anybody else, so we were our best friends. We hung out, we played with each other. And when we were in Korea, I seem to remember her being the good big sister. She took care of me."

As Roman and Diane grew older and made other friends they began to drift apart, though, as siblings do. In July 1987, the Chos moved to Richmond, where friends had told them it was less expensive to start a business. Mr. and Mrs. Cho opened a little mom-and-pop corner convenience store, KC Market, on West Leigh Street near Virginia Commonwealth University, a thriving urban college in the middle of the city's Fan District. An historic area that still had some cobblestone streets, it was populated with cheap restaurants, nightclubs, head shops and record stores that catered to the college kids. Telephone poles were plastered with artsy Xeroxed flyers advertising local music shows by acts like Richmond's notorious

Grammy-winning heavy metal band GWAR, which was just getting its start.

To her devoutly Christian mother, Diane Cho was the perfect daughter: smart, hard-working and ambitious. (*Photo courtesy Cho family*)

Like a lot of immigrant entrepreneurs, the Chos threw themselves into their business, working seven days a week, leaving early in the morning and often not getting home until as late as 9 o'clock at night.

As the Cho family's most proficient English speaker, 15-year-old Diane was saddled with responsibilities ranging from ordering stock for the convenience store to registering herself and her brother for school to handling everything at home like paying bills, looking after her brother and cooking and cleaning while her parents were away working.

"That's when my daughter, she kind of took charge," says Mrs. Cho, speaking through a court-certified Korean interpreter because she isn't a fluent English speaker. She still lives in South Side Richmond. Diane's father passed away from brain cancer in 2013.

"It was July when we moved from Maryland and we didn't know how to switch schools, we didn't know anything, but it was my daughter who ... got her brother [and] herself registered [for school]," Mrs. Cho remembers. "She was this person who almost became like our parent. She took care of the home business, and she was very savvy and she just did it without being told to do it."

As the children of immigrants, Diane and Roman had "responsibilities that a typical kid did not have," says Roman. "We had to figure out what was going on in this strange world that we were brought into. We had to take care of ourselves and sometimes take care of things that our parents should have been taking care of. If you ask any immigrant's kids, it's a common experience."

To her devoutly Christian mother, Diane was the perfect daughter: smart, hard-working and ambitious, with a playful sense of humor. She liked to sing and kept a sketchbook of drawings of still-life subjects like flowers.

"Her life goal was to become a doctor," Mrs. Cho says. "Whenever I get sick, she will say, 'Mom, just wait until I become a doctor. I will take good care of you.'"

But like a lot of 15-year-olds, Diane Cho was also starting to rebel in small ways.

"Around the time of when we moved to Virginia, we were definitely [in our] teenage years and we were at each other's throats. So we were not the best friends," remembers Roman.

Diane was trying her best to fit in with 1980s American teen culture. She had a scar about the size of a dime next to her left eyebrow from where doctors had removed a round birthmark. Sometimes kids made fun of her for that and her thick Korean accent.

"She was trying to wear the latest fashion, trying to do her hair in a certain way," says her brother. "And you can imagine that didn't go over too well with these parents who don't know the culture at all and who come from a rather traditional background. So there was the inevitable friction, just like [with] any kid who's becoming a teenager."

Seen here at age 15 in 1987, Diane Cho was beginning to rebel in small ways, smoking and dating a boy without her parents' knowledge. (*Photo courtesy Cho family*)

Diane adored fashion. She wore a jean jacket with metal studs and had dyed blonde streaks in her hair. She didn't drink or do drugs but she occasionally smoked cigarettes, which wasn't that unusual a form of rebellion for '80s teens. And she was also dating a local Korean boy without her parents' knowledge.

"It wasn't like [a] serious relationship or anything. So I don't think she told them about it," her best friend Jenny says, adding that Diane "was definitely a good kid. No trouble at school. It was just like, you know, [a] puberty kind of thing that, you know, I guess she tried smoking and stuff like that. ... Diane was very innocent."

Like Diane, Jenny was a fairly recent Korean immigrant. A grade ahead of Diane in high school, Jenny had lived in Richmond for about two of the three years her family had been in the United States. Her name is Ji-Un but "people called me Jenny because they couldn't pronounce my name."

Like the Chos, Jenny's parents owned and ran a small neighborhood grocery store. And Jenny also had a younger brother, who was best friends with Diane's brother, Roman.

The Han family's apartment was located directly above the Chos' ground-floor, corner unit in one of the three large, two-story apartment buildings on their U-shaped court. Jenny's bedroom was right over Diane's room on the far side of their building, facing a wooded area out back. Late at night, the two girls would remove the screens from their bedroom windows and lean out and chat with each other. It was during one of these sessions that Diane told Jenny about the dreams she'd been having about someone following her.

Because the Chos and Hans worked long hours away from home, their latchkey daughters were unsupervised most of the time.

"It's sad that all the parents were away so many hours from the kids because we were really like all over the place, you know? Because our parents weren't there," remembers Jenny, now a mother herself and living on the West Coast.

Bonded by their mutual culture and experience, Diane and Jenny were instant best friends and quickly became like sisters. "We just basically did everything together," Jenny says. "You know, riding bicycle[s] together, come home, eat together and hang out with friends together." They enjoyed talking about fashion and listening to Korean pop music.

Like a lot of the kids in their South Side neighborhood, Jenny and Diane also spent much of their spare time across Midlothian Turnpike at Cloverleaf Mall. They'd shop for clothes and cosmetics at the mall, which in 1996 would be the scene of a grisly double murder and robbery at the mall's dollar store. (Cloverleaf, which fell into a steady decline through the 1990s, closed in 2008 and was demolished in 2011. A super-sized Kroger grocery store, fast food restaurants and apartments now occupy the site.)

The two girls bought makeup and toiletries at the drugstore across the street from Cloverleaf at the Beaufont Plaza shopping center, where unbeknownst to them, the South Side Strangler had either purchased or shoplifted the Vaseline he utilized in the rape and murder of Dr. Susan Hellams.

Diane and her teenage friends frequented the popular Cloverleaf Mall, which was located across Midlothian Turnpike from their Chesterfield County apartment complex. South Side Strangler victim Debbie Davis had worked part-time at the mall's Waldenbooks store.

"We used to walk there going through back roads, sort of like [an] undeveloped area. So you know we walked there to go [a] faster way and then I guess later I found out that the [killer], he was, like, following us around," Jenny says.

On the night of Saturday, November 21, 1987, Diane's parents arrived home to their apartment around 9 p.m. and Diane's mother gave her a haircut.

"She asked me to cut her hair and I did, and she said, 'Oh, Mom, this is way too short!'" remembers Mrs. Cho. "She's kind of a girl who has a sense of fashion. She knows how to style [her] hair and she put her hairpin in and [then] she said, 'Oh wow, this is not bad. And I'm sorry that I told you it was too short,' and that was the last conversation. So that is still ringing inside my head."

After that, Diane cut her younger brother Roman's hair. And sometime between 11:30 p.m. and midnight, as her parents went to sleep in their bedroom, they could hear Diane in her room across the hall, typing out a homework assignment for her freshman English class.

Not long afterwards, maybe around 12:30 a.m. to 1 a.m., Diane opened her window and knocked on the outside wall of the apartment building to try to get Jenny's attention.

"I heard her knocking on the wall to talk to me [in the] middle of the night, but I couldn't open the window and talk to her because I was really ill and I wish I could have answered her or talked to her, but it didn't happen," recalls a rueful Jenny. "Funny thing is, I didn't hear *anything* except for her knocking on the wall."

The next day, on Sunday morning, Diane's parents left early for work. Their daughter's bedroom door was still closed.

"Teenage time, they want to sleep. So we didn't bother [waking her]," remembers Mrs. Cho.

Around 2 p.m., the Chos closed up their store so they could attend an afternoon church service. They called home at least two times to make sure their kids would be ready to go to church. Both times 12-year-old Roman answered the phone, telling his mother that he was watching TV and that Diane was still asleep.

"She called me several times," Roman says. "My mom kept asking me to go wake my sister up and my sister had a bit of a temper at the time. She would call and say, 'Go wake your sister up!' [and] I would say, 'No, no, no, I don't want to go in there. She's sleeping!'"

Finally, Mr. and Mrs. Cho drove back home to their apartment, arriving around 3 p.m.: "We said, 'Oh, you're still sleeping?' And then we opened the door."

"I heard my mom scream. It was my mom who found her," remembers Roman. "I guess it's a mother's instinct that my mom for some reason rushed into my sister's room."

"My daughter was wrapped in rope. Her face was purple and the window was open," says Diane's mother. "And then I started to untie her [but] my husband stopped me and said that might be evidence so don't touch it."

"When I walked in," Roman says, "my mom was untying the ropes that bound my sister. And I don't know if I tried to pull her away from doing that or if it was my dad. But I feel like somebody was trying to stop my mom from doing that. And at that point my mom was hysterical ... like undoing the ropes would bring my sister back."

Mrs. Cho fainted from shock not long after discovering her brutalized daughter's remains.

The pitiful young teen's body was face-down in her bed. Her hands had been bound behind her back and her ankles had also been tied together. She had been strangled with a slip-knot noose, which was still looped around her neck; her mouth was gagged with duct tape. Diane's cut-off sleep shorts were missing and the bed sheet was strategically draped over her buttocks. The killer had removed the bedroom window screen, which lay on the ground outside.

Diane's brother called 911 to report the murder: "I remember the operator asking me if I could administer CPR and me telling her that there wasn't any point; that she was dead."

Being largely unable to speak or read English and not really knowing anyone outside of their insular Korean church, Mr. and Mrs. Cho had never learned about the serial killer stalking Richmond.

The South Side Strangler had tortured, raped and murdered Diane while her parents and brother slept in the bedrooms right next to hers in the modest, three-bedroom apartment. None of them heard a thing.

"Our job is really taxing, so as soon as we hit the bed, it's like we're corpses, we're dead, as soon as we fall asleep. If somebody moved us, we wouldn't even know. If an earthquake happened, we wouldn't even know," remembers Mrs. Cho.

Upstairs, Jenny Han, who was still feeling ill, had stayed home while her parents went to church, and she began to hear a commotion in Diane's bedroom below.

"I hear someone cry so loud and then I put my ears on the floor," says Jenny, "and then … I felt like something really, really bad happened. So I just ran downstairs."

The Chos' apartment door was open "and then I just pushed [past] everybody in the room. And then I saw her mother crying in the living room and police officers all over," Jenny recalls tearfully. "I just, like, ran to her room and I saw her naked body on the bed against the wall. … I saw the back of her body. … I remember that I saw her hands tied but I didn't see her [face]. … And it was really quick because they dragged me out there not to see it."

Diane Cho's best friend, Jenny Han, lived in the apartment above Diane's. The two teens would talk to each other out of their bedroom windows at night.

Even decades removed from that day, Jenny still battles to block out her traumatic memories of it.

In the wake of her friend's murder, police questioned Jenny but she couldn't tell them anything about the killer, other than the fact that Diane told her she'd been having nightmares about someone following her. The detectives wanted to know everything about Diane – where she hung out and who her friends were.

Diane's boyfriend, who was ruled out as a suspect, was no longer in the picture. "He was having a hard time and he asked me out [on a date] because he misses Diane so much," remembers Jenny. She turned him down. They never talked again.

Stunned community members, including the local Korean-American association, immediately put up more than $6,000 in reward money for information leading to the arrest and conviction of Diane's murderer.

Some of the local Koreans, though, blamed *Jenny* for Diane's death, saying that if the girls hadn't been opening their windows to talk to each other in the first place, Diane wouldn't have been killed. Already experiencing survivor's guilt, Jenny blamed herself, too.

"It was really hard for me to take it. … I try to kill myself because I felt so guilty," she says, recounting her failed attempt at overdosing with over-the-counter pills. She also took up smoking, something she never did before.

"After that incident happened, I feel somewhat guilty because what if I would have answered her that night and make sure that she closed her window?" Jenny says. "Or I feel bad that it could have been me. [There are] a lot of guilty feelings involved."

The rest of high school was a tough time for Jenny, whose mother unexpectedly died from cancer two years after Diane was murdered. By that time, Jenny had turned to her Christian faith for solace. Rededicating herself to her studies, she decided to pursue a happy life for Diane's sake.

She firmly believes that she and her best friend will be reunited in Heaven, where Diane continues to watch over her.

"She's always next to me," says Jenny, who's now in her late 40s. "I have to live my life. I have to show her I'm doing good. … I love her and miss her. She['s] always in my heart. [I] cannot forget her."

❖

Thirty years later, Roman Cho says he doesn't feel guilty that he and his parents didn't hear the murder taking place, "just incredibly saddened and in horror that it happened one room away the whole time and we didn't know about it."

So how *did* the Strangler kill Diane in a bedroom surrounded by sleeping family members without waking anyone up? Retired Richmond homicide detective Ray Williams believes that the killer promptly took control of the frightened teenager, covering her mouth with duct tape and threatening to kill her or her family if she made any noise: "He's probably in there before she got home and immediately, he probably told her, 'I'm not going to hurt you, just do I as say,' and he put duct tape on her [mouth] and tied her hands around her back."

Diane Cho's murder bore all the hallmarks of the South Side Strangler's killings of Debbie Davis and Susan Hellams but there were also some key differences. For one, this murder happened in neighboring Chesterfield County, still south of the James River, but about a four- to five-mile drive west from the South Richmond neighborhoods where the Strangler had previously struck. Also, Diane's body was found with a crudely drawn, lopsided figure eight or infinity sign painted on her left thigh in red nail polish. And unlike Davis and Hellams, who had been home alone, Diane's entire family was in the apartment at the time she was killed.

Serial killers generally escalate, starting out with lesser criminal acts such as window peeping, burglary, or arson and working their way up to crimes against persons, such as robbery, rape and increasingly violent murders.

The South Side Strangler's *modus operandi* was remarkably similar to that of the Golden State Killer, a serial killer who terrorized California in the 1970s and 1980s, killing at least 13 people and raping more than 50 women and teenage girls. In April, based on a DNA match, California police arrested 72-year-old Joseph DeAngelo, a former police officer, for the murders.

"I'm sure he started as a peeping Tom and then he went to, 'I wonder what it would be like to be inside a house.' And he then he went onto, 'I wonder what it would be like to take some stuff,' and then really ransacking the houses and then encountering people," says investigative journalist and true-crime blogger Billy Jensen, who helped complete Michelle McNamara's posthumously published bestseller, *I'll Be Gone in the Dark: One Woman's Obsessive Search for the Golden State Killer.*

Speaking about the Golden State Killer, Jensen could easily be discussing the South Side Strangler: "He liked being in their house. He liked to maintain that terror. He didn't just go in and rape somebody; he would go in, rape them and then go in their kitchen and eat food and eat crackers and drink beer and then come back and steal stuff. He very much was going in their house saying, 'I'm king here. This is my house now for the next two or three hours and I can do whatever the hell I want'"

Given the pattern of the other South Side Strangler murders and the fact that Diane's parents were so often away from the apartment, at least one former FBI agent who assisted on the case thinks it's possible that the Strangler may have mistaken Diane for a young adult who lived alone. Maybe he didn't know there were other family members in the apartment.

Or, maybe he was just getting overly confident as he kept killing without consequence. That would fit the pattern of other serial killers, according to Louis Schlesinger, Ph.D., a professor of forensic psychology at John Jay College of Criminal Justice in New York who is the author of books on sexual murders and compulsive homicides.

"They don't want to be caught but they do get more reckless, particularly if they kill a number of people and don't get caught because they feel that they're going to outsmart law enforcement," Schlesinger says. "And so you often find that, at the end of a killing cycle, they tend to get careless, they tend to get reckless. They do things not to get caught, they don't want to get caught, but they often do things to ensure that they *will* get caught – like entering a home and raping and killing somebody while other family members are there or communicating with the police and sending them letters and this sort of thing. So that's not atypical at all."

The most notable difference between this killing and the earlier murders, however, was the fact that, unlike the other victims, Diane was Korean and a teenager, not a white, middle-aged woman. The state medical examiner would determine that Diane had been a virgin at the time of the attack. She had suffered lacerations and tears to her vagina and hymen. Menstrual blood and semen were found on the woven orange blanket and bed sheets in Diane's bedroom. The top of her head was also bruised.

A hair recovered by lab techs from the linens at the scene was thought to belong to a person of African descent. As with the murders of Debbie Davis and Susan Hellams, there were no fingerprints found and there were no signs of a struggle. Virtually nothing in Diane's bedroom had been disturbed, though a few items were discovered to be missing: the shorts she had been wearing, the bottle of red nail polish used to paint the figure 8 on her thigh and a photo of Diane that had been removed from a frame.

As soon as Chesterfield County Police investigators finished processing the scene, they contacted their counterparts in Richmond.

"Chesterfield called the next day: 'Hey, Ray, you might want to come over here,'" recalls Ray Williams. And as soon as he walked into the scene, he thought to himself, "Uh-oh, we're looking for the same guy."

Chesterfield assigned two detectives to the case: Ernest Hazzard and Bill Showalter, both of whom have passed away in the intervening years. Hazzard and Showalter would serve with the Williams Boys on the inter-agency task force devoted to catching the South Side Strangler. But regional cooperation wasn't the rule in those days. While Hazzard and Showalter were more than happy to accept outside help on the difficult case, Williams says, not everyone on the county police department was lining up to hold hands and sing "Kumbaya" with the city police – even with a serial killer at large.

"They had a grouchy ass lieutenant," Ray remembers. While working on the Cho murder, he says, that lieutenant accused Williams of putting a bumper sticker on the lieutenant's unmarked police car that read, "Of all the things I've lost, I miss my mind the most." The lieutenant went so far as to task a forensics technician with dusting the sticker for fingerprints.

"I said, 'Lieutenant, No. 1, I don't work for you. And No. 2, with my experience, wouldn't you think I would put gloves on if I put [the bumper sticker] on [your car]?'" Ray says.

"Yeah, I didn't tell him it was me."

That same Monday morning that Ray Williams was at the Cho murder scene, there was an empty desk at Manchester High School.

Ninth-grade English teacher Ellen Young had been out of town visiting family the weekend Diane was murdered and hadn't seen the news. When she arrived at work that Monday morning, she overheard her colleagues in the teacher's lounge discussing something tragic that had happened.

"I heard somebody say something about whose student was she? And I was like, 'What are you guys talking about?' And they said, 'The South Side Strangler guy, he struck again and killed another person. And it was a student here.' They said [it was] a little Korean girl [but they] didn't remember what her name was. And then I knew. And that was just right before I had to go in my classroom. I was just floored."

It was Young's first year working as a teacher and Diane Cho had been in her class for a little under three months. Young recalls "not knowing what to do in a classroom for 50 minutes with a bunch of kids who had one of their friends killed and killed horrendously. It was kind of a defining moment for me with my teaching, I can tell you that."

Young also remembers a bone-chilling chat she had with Diane one afternoon not long before the murder. While serving a detention for being tardy, Diane had told Ellen about how she and Jenny would talk to each other out of their windows at night.

"I remember looking at her saying, 'Diane, you can't do this anymore. There's a crazy guy out there killing people and coming into their apartments.' And she smiled, and I know this is going to sound dramatic and it shouldn't, but, right then, a shaft of sunlight came through my classroom window and it completely illuminated her face. And I remember looking at it and right then being struck [with the thought that] she's not going to shut that window. And she didn't."

As word spread about the killing that Sunday, many of Diane's neighbors gathered in the apartment parking lot and watched as the medical examiner's staff wheeled a stretcher out of the building with Diane's body, wrapped in a white sheet. News footage from the moment shows Mrs. Cho wailing on the concrete steps, as she's gently held back by a plainclothes police officer.

Some of the neighbors who had been there were Ellen Young's students and Diane's classmates. "There was a lot of trauma for a lot of my kids who lived in that apartment complex with her," Young says.

A week or two after the murder, one of Young's students approached her and said that Desi Fierros knew something about the killing. Desi and Diane were both students in the same freshman English class taught by Young.

"I was shocked," Young says, "and I said, 'Well, [Desi] has to go to the police,' and the kid says, 'She doesn't want to go to the police. She's not going to go unless you go with her,' which was kind of shocking."

After speaking with Desi, Young immediately arranged a meeting with police.

Desi was a tough, street-smart Puerto Rican kid who had recently moved to Chesterfield from New York City and she saw in Diane a fellow outsider. They rode the school bus together and when other kids picked on Diane, Desi would stand up to them.

It had taken a little while for Desi to connect the dots between the murder and the incident at the Cloverleaf Mall multiplex, when Diane had pointed out her stalker. "I just didn't think or connect at that point ... that [he] may have been the serial killer. I was only 15. My mind didn't work like that," Desi says. "[It was] one of the scariest things I've ever gone through in my life."

After Desi revealed to her mother that she thought she had seen Diane's killer, her mother accused her of lying and warned her not to get involved, forbidding her to talk to the police.

Nevertheless, Desi pressed ahead and she and her English teacher say they met with two Chesterfield County police detectives and a sketch artist at the school.

"I didn't think twice about defying my mother to do it because, well, that was just me back then," Desi says. "I was quite rebellious and mad and pissed off at the world that she had made me move to Virginia from New York, you know, and so I was just really impossible."

And what's more, Desi trusted Ellen Young, who held her hand while she gave her statement to police.

Desi told the Chesterfield detectives that the man she saw had been "wearing a blue shirt. His shirt was like an Izod-type shirt with a collar. He had on khaki pants, like a uniform [with] boots, and he was a light-skinned black man," remembers Desi, now a mother of six and living in Puerto Rico. "The police looked at me, looked at each other, looked at Ellen and then looked back at me. I thought because I had said he was a black man [that] they thought I was lying."

Ray Williams doesn't recall hearing about this interview from the Chesterfield detectives and Desi was never called to testify in court. The Chesterfield County Police Department did not respond to multiple requests for any records that might exist from an interview with Desi. No sketch of a suspect was ever released to the media.

One former FBI agent says that Desi had probably conflated later news coverage of the killer with her actual memories of Diane and that she never really saw the Strangler.

However, Ellen Young independently corroborates Desi's account of what she told the police – and the fact that the interview took place while the Strangler was still at large.

"It was a life-changing thing for both me and Desi," Young says. "And I think it defined a lot of what Desi is as a person as far as being honest and what's right and what's wrong. Desi kind of broke the code, you know? This is not something you do in their culture. You did not go to cops. *You did not do this.* But Desi did it because Diane was her friend and that was the right thing to do. That was the moment of truth there for that kid."

Meanwhile, the Chos were left to deal with their grief and fear. Just as Tolstoy said that all unhappy families are unhappy in their own way, the same could also be said of families shattered by violence.

"Our whole family was frightened," Roman says. "I remember right afterward there was the period when my parents, they took the mattress and put it in the living room and we, the three of us, slept together for a while. And it wasn't anything that was spoken about or said. It was just something that we did."

In the weeks afterwards, Roman found himself "just thinking about how just a short moment ago or just a day ago or just a week ago, everything was fine and how I wish that we could go back to that week. And at the same time, fully understanding what had happened – and just being in disbelief about it."

"I just wanted to follow my daughter to [the] grave," recalls Diane's mother, Hyun Kyoung Cho. "That's how I felt. I couldn't stop crying. When I go to a wedding, I would cry. I go to a funeral, I would cry. I cried nonstop for three years."

At work, she says, "My husband would go to the storeroom, the inventory room, and hold on to [the] cash register and cry. We tried to hide from each other that we're crying."

Speaking to a *Richmond Times-Dispatch* reporter in May 1989, with a Korean friend acting as his interpreter, Diane and Roman's father, Jong Chul Cho, said, "We are sad even today. We try to forget the death. But it will be [a long time] before we can forget it. ... Our dream is all broken."

Jong Chul Cho would sometimes tell his wife that Diane was never meant to be their daughter, that they were never meant to be her parents.

"It broke my dad," Roman remembers. "My impression of him as I grew up, as I went through high school, college and became an adult, was that he seemed to be a broken man. There was never a sense of happiness in our family."

Roman still struggles with the fact that he and Diane weren't getting along at the time of her murder. He wonders if they would have reconciled and grown closer as they got older, like Jenny Han and her brother have. Roman never had any counseling following the murder and he sometimes tells people that he was an only child because it's easier than trying to explain the painful truth about his family.

"I don't know what the right answer is whenever people ask me that question because every time I say I'm the only kid, I am erasing my sister's memory. I'm erasing my sister from history," Roman says. "I'd forgotten what her voice sounded like quite a while back. I can't remember. I can't recall that all. I'm starting to basically forget what she looked like."

In 30 years, Roman says, "this is the most I've spoken about my sister and there's a lot of things that I've said for the first time."

Immediately following Diane's murder, the three Chos relocated to a different apartment in the same complex, this time on the second floor. Roman and his mother never set foot in the old apartment after the day Diane's body was found.

The Chos' new apartment had an identical floor plan to their old unit; the bedroom that would have belonged to Diane instead became a guest room where Roman's grandmother stayed when she visited from Maryland.

And at age 12, Roman suddenly had to take on all of his late sister's responsibilities for the family. "After she passed away," he says, "there were times when my dad would ask about what this bill would mean, where he would get a bill from like gas and power and he couldn't make it out. So I'm trying to figure that out, kind of understand what this letter is talking about and that's something that my sister went through from the time she was 12 when we first came to the U.S."

Everything Diane owned was either confiscated by police or thrown away by the friends and church members who cleaned out the Chos' old apartment. Jenny Han's parents also threw out all of Diane's clothes and other belongings that Jenny had borrowed. The Han family moved out after the murder too, leaving for a different apartment complex entirely.

"My parents just got rid of everything," says Jenny, whose parents also didn't allow her to attend Diane's funeral service. In Korean culture, she explains, "you're not supposed to keep the dead people's items or anything. And so they just got rid of everything. And that really upset me at that time. It was very painful for me. They took Diane's clothing, everything away from me. I don't have anything."

A couple weeks after the murder, the *Richmond Times-Dispatch* reported that Diane's bedroom remained half-empty. The mattress she was killed on was shoved upright against one wall. Some clothes were still hanging in her closet and a little nightstand in the room was bestrewn with makeup, nail polish and cassette tapes. A dead rose was left on the ground outside Diane's bedroom window, apparently left by one of her friends as an impromptu tribute to the slain teen.

Roman wishes his family had kept his sister's art toolkit and her pencil sketches. He also would like to have inherited her treasured hard-back copy of the Laura Ingalls Wilder novel *Little House on the Prairie*. It had been a gift from her best friend in Maryland before the Cho family relocated to Richmond. That friend, a Vietnamese teen, phoned the Cho household not long after the murder and asked to speak with Diane. "And I had to tell her that my sister had passed away," Roman says. "That was difficult news to deliver and I'm sure it was a huge shock to this girl."

As for Diane's mother, she only has about three photographs of Diane left. They're all loaded on her smartphone. In one picture, Diane's smiling, wearing a white t-shirt with a brightly colored '80s-style design. In another, she's wearing a sleeveless, pastel yellow dress for a church Easter service. Chesterfield police confiscated the rest of the photos Diane's family had and never returned them, Hyun Kyoung Cho says.

"This is the only picture I carry of my daughter," she says, clasping a small photo. "And she just stays the same and the picture doesn't change. If she was alive, she would have changed. She was very smart back then. Can you imagine how smart she would be now?

"I mean can you imagine if my daughter's here? I wouldn't end up like this if my daughter was around," says Diane's mother, who now lives by herself in the Richmond area, where she is a member of a Korean-American Christian church.

"She kind of sort of took care of everything, and living in America, with the language barrier that I have, she would have taken care of everything. Right now I would not have any trouble living here if my daughter was around. Probably a lot of problems I have right now I wouldn't have if she's here.

"I miss her so much. She was such a smart girl."

CHAPTER 4

HER LAST DEBT

That was odd, thought Audrey Sizelove.

Pulling into the U-shaped court of brick townhouses where they lived in suburban Arlington, Virginia, Audrey and her husband had been returning from their Thanksgiving weekend travels that Sunday evening, November 29, 1987, when Audrey noticed that her neighbor Sue Tucker's corner townhome was dark. As far as Audrey knew, though, Sue was supposed to be home.

And there was something else even more unusual, especially given the frosty chill in the air: "I noticed right away as soon as we got back that the window to her bedroom was open," recalls Audrey. "I thought that was strange because I had never seen that [window] open before."

Sue Tucker, 44, worked as a magazine editor for the U.S. Department of Agriculture. She and her husband, Reg, had been neighbors with the Sizeloves in the townhome community of Fairlington Villages since the early 1980s, when the Tuckers first moved to Arlington, located just outside of Washington, D.C., and about 100 miles north of the state capital in Richmond.

Reg had worked as a photographer for the Fairfax County, Virginia, school system but in August he had taken a job as a photography teacher at a university back in his native country of Wales. Sue was preparing to join him there – she had just returned from visiting Reg a couple weeks before but she'd had to return to

Virginia to sell their townhouse and wrap up some projects at work before she could leave.

Sue and Reg Tucker were typical residents of Fairlington Villages, a friendly neighborhood largely populated by federal employees and contractors. Constructed during World War II by the U.S. government to house defense workers and their families, Fairlington Villages was the largest apartment complex in the nation at the time it was built. During the 1970s, its 3,439 units were converted to townhouses and condominiums. Every month or so, the women in the court where the Tuckers lived would get together for a potluck dinner. They also pitched in to help one another: Because Sue didn't drive, Audrey and her husband had gladly volunteered to help Sue out with errands like taking her to buy groceries at the local Safeway store after Reg left for Wales.

Sue Tucker was preparing to move with her husband, Reg, to his native country of Wales at the time of her murder. (*Photo courtesy Reg Tucker*)

Sue was supposed to go to grocery shopping with the Sizeloves that Monday evening, November 30. She usually called them the night or morning before, but the Sizeloves hadn't heard from her. And she didn't answer her phone when Audrey tried calling.

"We normally went to the grocery store on Monday, so at some point I called her and she didn't pick up, so I left a message and I never heard from her," Audrey Sizelove says. "At that point then I started really getting concerned about her well-being."

Early the next morning, Tuesday, December 1, 1987, Audrey drove her husband to the airport so he could catch a plane to Texas for a business trip. She tried calling Sue again. Still no answer. Tuesday evening, Sue's townhouse remained dark. And her second-floor bedroom window was still open.

A neighbor noticed that Sue Tucker's upstairs bedroom window had been open for days in chilly late November 1987.

Audrey had a spare key to Sue's house from when Sue had visited Wales earlier that month, so she decided to check on her and make sure nothing was wrong. She asked their neighbor Kathy to accompany her. The two women stood on the concrete porch of the Tuckers' large, box-like brick duplex while Audrey unlocked and opened the door ... which abruptly halted. The chain lock was fastened from inside.

"I was pretty certain she was in there," Audrey says, "I wasn't thinking, 'Oh god, something's happened,' but I was getting more concerned. And so we went around the back and I crawled up on the back balcony and the back door was [cracked] open. And I pushed it open and I might have stepped inside just one or two steps and I thought, well, I'm not going any further because something isn't right and I think I noticed an odor at that point."

It was the scent of "rotting flesh. It was just pretty bad."

The two women returned to Kathy's house, where Audrey called the police.

Back in the mid- to late 1980s, Arlington only had a handful of killings each year, mostly domestic murders. So you'd think a bondage rape and murder would be a first for this Washington, D.C., bedroom community.

Only, it wasn't.

Retired Arlington Detective Bob Carrig doesn't remember that many details of his old cases anymore, but he does recall *exactly* what he told fellow homicide detective Joe Horgas that night at the Sue Tucker murder scene: "It's Carolyn Hamm all over again."

Says Carrig: "I told Joe that night when we were at the Tucker [murder scene], you know, we've seen this *before*."

Back in January 1984, 32-year-old Washington, D.C., attorney Carolyn Hamm was found face-down, nude, bound and strangled to death in the garage of her Arlington home. Carrig had worked that case. David Vasquez, a mentally challenged fast food worker and former school janitor, had confessed to the murder and was serving a 35-year prison sentence for it.

So why were they seeing an almost identical murder scene three years later and less than a mile away at Sue Tucker's townhome?

The patrol officers who'd first responded to Audrey Sizelove's emergency 911 call that Tuesday evening had also climbed over the black metal railings and onto the back balcony of Sue Tucker's townhouse. They observed that someone had braced a chair against the unlocked back door from the inside, but it wasn't heavy enough to prevent entry into the home.

As the officers peered inside by the glow of their sweeping flashlights, the beams illuminated an empty pocketbook, its contents scattered haphazardly at the bottom of a staircase. They unholstered their guns and forced their way inside.

"Police officers!" they called out. "We are entering with our weapons drawn! If anyone is present, make your presence known immediately!"

Upstairs, in the master bedroom, the officers found Sue Tucker's badly decomposing nude body lying face-down lengthwise across her bed, tightly trussed with glossy white nylon ropes. A pool of viscous, dark crimson liquid had collected on the comforter and the floor beneath her head. The killer had covered her buttocks with a dark blue polyester sleeping bag.

Medical examiners would later determine that Sue Tucker had been vaginally and anally raped, finding evidence of spermatozoa in swabs from both areas. Unusually large amounts of the killer's semen were also discovered on the sleeping bag and a nightgown.

"The body itself wasn't pretty. I mean, she'd been laying there for several days and the skin had bubbles under it. ... It just didn't look good. She was turning black," remembers retired Arlington County Police homicide detective Joe Horgas, who was the lead investigator on the Tucker murder case. A thickset former high school football player and family man with a hearty laugh and a slight Northern accent from his native Pennsylvania, Horgas had been a homicide and robbery detective for nine of the 19 years he had worked so far on the small suburban police force. And this would be far and away the biggest case of his career.

From what Horgas could ascertain, the murderer had brought the ropes with him, demonstrating premeditation. And Tucker had been bound in an almost identical fashion to 1984 victim Carolyn Hamm. The killer had even used the same reef and half-hitch knots to secure the bindings.

"Her hands were tied behind her back and there was a rope going from her hands to her neck … so that if you could keep your hands up long enough towards your head, you could keep the pressure from choking yourself," Horgas explains. Exhausted and in too much pain, the victim would inevitably surrender to the rope's unyielding pressure and be strangled.

Struck by the obvious similarities between the two murders, "I was anxious to get back to the police department to rip open the Hamm case and to learn everything I could about it," recalls Horgas. "One [killing] was on one side of Walter Reed Drive, the other was on the other side of [Walter Reed] Drive in the same general [geographic] area and all the M.O. was the same: the hands tied behind the back, rope around the neck, the purse strewn around the floor."

Regardless, it wasn't going to be an easy crime to solve – that much was certain.

Lab techs at the Tucker murder scene couldn't find any fingerprints from the killer, who had broken in through a small, narrow window in the basement laundry room at the rear of the townhouse, which backed up to a small field at the edge of a wooded area on a dead-end road. (Later, a lean, 6-foot-plus Arlington police officer would squeeze through the impossibly tiny-looking 13-inch wide by 16-inch high laundry room window to prove it could be done, while Horgas photographed the feat for evidence.)

Broken glass lay scattered on the orange laundry room rug, near two lengths of the same bright white nylon rope that had been used to bind and strangle Sue Tucker. Forensics officers found evidence that the killer had used a cloth to wipe down the washing machine below the window, probably to obscure any possible fingerprints or shoeprints.

The next day, when she was out walking her dog in the field behind the townhouse, Audrey Sizelove found a blue washcloth snagged on a tree branch. She carefully retrieved it without touching it, bagged it and turned it over to police. Lab techs would discover pubic hair from a person of African descent on the washcloth, which was determined to be taken from the Tucker residence. (Sue Tucker had a habit of keeping a washcloth in upstairs bathroom's shower but there wasn't a washcloth there when her body was found.) Police would find similar pubic hairs on Sue Tucker's bathroom counter and sink as well as on a blanket in the bedroom.

There was one other detail from the Sue Tucker murder scene that Horgas found particularly galling – and disturbing. In the dining area downstairs, police discovered a serrated kitchen knife and a half-eaten orange sitting out on the dining room table. Sue Tucker had kept a neat house; she had had taken time and care painting and preparing the two-bedroom townhouse for sale and making sure it was presentable. She wouldn't have cut an orange on the table without first putting it on a plate or cutting board.

Clearly, the killer had taken time to fix himself a snack before leaving.

"We don't know, but we suspected it was the suspect put it there," says Horgas. "I believe there was a bite taken out of it or something and I know we tried to get teeth-mark comparisons and stuff like that, but it was too deteriorated. It had been sitting too long."

"He was inside the home for quite some time – it wasn't just a very quick in-and-out type of situation. Many of the drawers had been ransacked, had been gone through," retired Arlington detective Rick Schoembs said of the killer in an episode of the popular true-crime documentary cable TV series *Forensic Files*.

For Helen Fahey, Arlington County's elected prosecutor at the time, the case hit too close to home – literally.

"I had been living [in Fairlington Villages] up until a few months before this happened," she recollects. "The community is mainly composed of these very small World War II townhouses, [a] very, very pleasant community. ... The townhouses are all laid out the same and the one that I had been living in was in effect a mirror image of the house where the victim was found, so it gave me some things to think about.

"It was an unusual murder for Arlington. This is generally a very quiet community. There aren't a lot of homicides and there are very few homicides like that. And someone had gotten in through a window, which means almost anyone and everyone is vulnerable."

The medical examiner's office was only able to give a rough estimate of when the murder had taken place, probably 48 to 72 hours before the body was found. But aside from the killer, one other person was pretty certain of the time period when Sue had been murdered – her husband, Reg Tucker.

Reg and Sue would usually arrange to call each other early in the morning and late at night to save money on overseas long-distance phone charges.

They had last spoken at 6:30 p.m. Eastern time on November 27, 1987, the Friday after Thanksgiving; Reg had called her because it was 11:30 p.m. in Wales. Sue was excited – she had sold their townhome, she told her husband, and she'd be moving to Wales as soon as the sale closed! They arranged to speak again in three days at 6 a.m. Eastern the following Monday morning, when Sue would call Reg.

The call never came.

Reg called home that evening at 6 p.m. but Sue didn't pick up. And then he called again. And again.

By Tuesday morning, December 1, Reg was extremely worried. By that evening, he was frantic. He started calling every 15 minutes. Then every 10 minutes. Then every minute.

The phone just rang and rang.

Then he just kept calling – for almost four straight hours.

At 1 a.m. on December 2 in Wales, about 7 p.m. Eastern time on December 1 in Virginia, Reg called Sue's cousin, Cyril Jackson, who lived nearby in Maryland, and asked him to check on her. Jackson said he would but Reg didn't hear anything back.

Two hours later, at about 9 p.m. Eastern time, Reg got a busy signal from the townhouse in Arlington. He kept calling until it rang again.

About 10 minutes later, an unfamiliar man's voice answered the phone.

"It was kind of an insolent man's voice," Reg recounts in his lilting Liverpudlian, Scouse accent, "and he said, 'What do you want?' And I said, 'I want to talk to Sue, I maybe got the wrong number.' And he said, 'No, she's not here,' and he hung up and [so] I called again."

This time, another man answered; he identified himself as Arlington Police Detective Rick Schoembs.

"He just said, 'Take a seat.' I knew. ... I didn't need to take a seat. I knew what it was, and he said, 'Your wife is dead,'" recalls Tucker, the devastation of the moment still painfully clear in his voice. "It was a nightmare finding out about her."

Reg and Sue Tucker had been married 18 years.

"Sue was amazing. She was a very trusting and very gentle person. She was just amazing, such a gentle person, such a lovely soul," says her widower. "We met in the U.K., when we were both at art school in London and we met there. We were together for two years before we got married."

The Tuckers spent the 1970s living in Arizona, where Sue worked for the U.S. Forest Service. Sue took her Department of Agriculture job in D.C. in the early 1980s, when the couple moved to Arlington. They traveled extensively on vacations, sometimes to visit Sue's parents and sister, who lived in Brazil, sometimes to Wales to see Reg's family.

An artist at heart, Sue usually kept a sketchbook during their travels. "If we took a vacation somewhere," Reg says, "she'd sit and draw the scenes in front of her. She'd draw people."

Sue and Reg enjoyed their life in Arlington, often socializing with Sue's cousin and his wife, but by the late 1980s, the vibe in America was changing and the Tuckers were ready to leave.

Ironically, the couple had decided to move back to the United Kingdom "because of the violence in the States. We were worried about crime," Reg Tucker remembers. "We just thought that in general people are much more relaxed in Wales, so [we wanted] to go back into a more relaxed society. She came and visited a few [weeks] before she was killed. And she stayed maybe two weeks and then she went back to finish up some work at her [job] and to sell the house."

Reg and Sue Tucker at Sue's cousin's home, 1987 (*Photo courtesy Reg Tucker*)

Sue had taken pride in editing the U.S. Department of Agriculture's news and research magazine, Reg says, and at the time of her murder, she was busy putting the finishing touches on what she intended to be her final articles for the publication, a piece about gypsy moths and a story about a possible link between sphagnum moss and cancer.

As soon as he found out about Sue's murder, Reg took the first possible flight back to D.C., accompanied by his brother. "I was just a mess, a complete mess. I was a mess all the way through the flight," he remembers.

"To make matters worse," Reg says bitterly, "they interrogated me at the airport in the States. I suppose they thought it was suspicious that I was crying, so they took me into a room and interrogated me."

A retired photography professor now living in Canada, Reg still deeply resents the way he says he was treated by police following his wife's murder. He alleges that Horgas interrogated him multiple times, treating him like a murder suspect and doing insensitive things like dumping out the contents of Sue's purse on a table in front of him.

However, Horgas denies this version of events and says he never suspected Reg for several reasons – including the fact that Reg had been overseas when the murder occurred and also because the case was so clearly connected to the Carolyn Hamm murder from three years earlier.

"I mean, he was never a suspect. I don't know where he's … that flabbergasts me. He was never, _never_ a suspect in her death," maintains Horgas.

In the immediate aftermath of Sue Tucker's murder, Horgas says, his attention was largely focused on one man and one man alone: David Vasquez, the prisoner who was serving time for murdering Carolyn Hamm.

Back in 1984, Carrig and others in the department had theorized that Vasquez must have had an accomplice in the young attorney's murder. So Horgas immediately reviewed the Hamm murder file and traveled to interview Vasquez in prison, with the objective of trying to figure out who had helped him kill Carolyn Hamm.

Horgas was authorized to offer Vasquez his freedom if he would help police apprehend Sue Tucker's killer, but "he just didn't come across as having done it," the detective says. "We were in the warden's office at the penitentiary and it seemed like we talked for an hour and a half and it was like spinning your wheels and not going anywhere.

"He just didn't know anything."

In the meantime, Reg Tucker may have gotten closer to the killer than the investigators. After the police finished processing the Tucker townhouse, Reg decided he would stay a few days there to be alone with his memories of Sue.

That's when he received the phone call.

"Mr. Tucker?" a man's voice asked on the other end of the line.

"Speaking," Reg answered.

"No, _Mrs. Tucker_. She's not there, is she?"

And then Reg says, the caller "kind of laughed. And he hung up." The grieving widower says he reported the call to Horgas, but "he just brushed it off. He said, 'Oh, it was just an advertising call, just a nuisance call,'" charges Reg. "He just completely brushed it off."

Reg Tucker is 100 percent positive that the caller was the killer taunting him and he faults police for failing to take it seriously: "It was him. I'm absolutely certain."

Horgas has no memory of the incident.

Sue Tucker's remains were cremated. Reg took half of her ashes to her family in South America and scattered the remaining ashes near where they had lived in Arizona, "at a place we call Sacred Mountain and it was down near Sedona, between Sedona and Camp Verde."

That marked the start of decades of difficult years for Reg, grappling alone with his anger and grief.

"I used to teach three to four days a week. I used to be, like, you know, the happy guy at work and I'd come home and cry all night," he remembers. "And this went on for years and years."

Reg also dealt with the murder in his art. In 1996 he published a book of his photos called *Seeing the Hours*, which features portraits taken by Reg capturing moments frozen in time, with people all around the world waiting in lines, waiting for loved ones – perpetually *waiting* for something that would never happen.

"The photographs were all people who were waiting and who'd gone into themselves," he explains, "and a lot of people said that it was a very depressing book. There are no smiling faces in it."

These days, Reg is coping with the recent loss of another woman he loved, his partner Gayle, who had helped him finally achieve some measure of peace. "I was really angry until maybe five years ago, I'd say [for] a good 25 years," he says, until "I met [Gayle] in 2009 and we worked together and she helped me get through it. We talked about it quite a bit and she helped me laugh again. I feel like I've come to terms with it. I can't undo it. I just feel that [Sue] has found peace. So in a way, in a way I've kind of accepted it.

"At that time when I met [Gayle], I was making images that were very angry and about violence to women and, through Gayle's help, I learned to laugh again. ... [But] in January 2016 she was diagnosed with a very aggressive form of lymphoma. She did chemo and she died last August."

Gayle's death is yet another trauma for him, Reg says, but not too long ago he had a dream in which he felt enveloped in a perfect sense of peace, love, calm and security. He thinks it was a message from Gayle, still looking after him.

He hasn't felt the same sort of presence from Sue, but he believes there's a reason for that.

"I don't know if I believe in nirvana," he says, "but Sue was such an incredible person. And after the murder, I did get some help from a psychologist or psychiatrist, and he said to me, 'Do you believe in angels?' and at the time, I didn't know ... but one thing he put to me is that maybe Sue, in paying this price, was paying her last debt.

"And that's what I think; I think that she is totally free now – that her spirit has moved on to another stage."

CHAPTER 5

A.K.A THE MASKED RAPIST

The community was under siege.

For months, a maniac had been on the loose, attacking women in their homes. And police had no suspects.

They called him … the Masked Rapist.

It all started in an Arlington, Virginia, grocery store parking lot at around 1 a.m. on June 27, 1983.

A 23-year-old woman was walking to her car after using a payphone when she was suddenly accosted by a skinny, young black man in his late teens or early 20s, who pointed a long knife at her face. He had pulled a white t-shirt over his head as a makeshift mask; his eyes glared out at her from its roughly cut holes. He got into her car and ordered her to drive, constantly threatening to stab her if she tried anything funny.

After 15 minutes he directed her to pull her car over at the end of a small cul-de-sac off South Oxford Street in Arlington's historically African-American Green Valley neighborhood. The dead end abruptly terminated into an empty wooded lot with a path leading into the dense, dark foliage. South Oxford was a hilly, well-populated street dotted with brick townhomes, but the car was hidden enough from the main road not to attract attention.

After searching the car's glove compartment for valuables, the masked man marched the hapless woman at knifepoint into the nearby forest, where he sexually assaulted her and commanded her to take off her clothes. When she refused, he sliced open her blouse. Once she had been made to disrobe, the masked man raped her twice, without ejaculating. He then told her he was going to her car to retrieve something and would return.

Thankfully, he never did, and the woman was able to escape after realizing the rapist had departed.

A slew of increasingly sadistic attacks would swiftly follow over the weeks and months to come.

Just two weeks after that June attack, the same masked man broke into another 23-year-old woman's Arlington apartment. Brandishing a 12-inch serrated knife in his gloved hand, he directed the frightened young woman to bring him her purse. After robbing her, he forced her to perform oral sex on him before raping her. The entire time, he kept up a compulsive patter of death threats and obscenities. If she didn't orgasm, he'd kill her, he promised. This M.O. would become a familiar story to police as the attacks continued to pile up.

As July gave way to August, two separate women had close calls with the Masked Rapist, narrowly escaping attempted abductions in their cars, but another young woman wasn't as fortunate.

On August 6, 1983, in the adjoining city of Alexandria, just outside Washington, D.C., the Masked Rapist forced a 22-year-old woman to drive her vehicle to a wooded area. Once there, he covered her eyes with silver duct tape and brutally sexually assaulted and raped her for more than two hours. He then introduced another new element to his crimes: tightly binding the young woman's hands behind her back with rope, he frog-marched her back to her car and forced her into the trunk.

After a few minutes, she began smelling smoke.

"I kicked and kicked as hard as I could," she would later tell police. "God must have been looking down because the trunk popped open. When I got out, fire was shooting out of the backseat."

Less than two weeks later, on August 17, the masked attacker abducted a 27-year-old woman at knifepoint from the laundry room of her Arlington apartment building. This time he wore socks on his hands instead of gloves. Once back in the woman's apartment, he engaged in his usual compulsive ritual of robbery, threats, sexual assault and rape. He brought along duct tape, which he used to gag her mouth, and he bound her hands and feet with found items from the apartment, such as a belt and a phone cord. Derisively, he told the woman, his only African-American victim, that he had been looking for a "white girl" instead of her.

After two more failed car abductions, on August 28, 1983, the Masked Rapist climbed into the open window of an apartment belonging to a 29-year-old Arlington woman before duct-taping her mouth and raping her. He also cut the cord from her Venetian blinds. A little over two weeks later, on September 18, he would rape a 22-year-old Arlington woman in virtually identical fashion, also entering her apartment through an open window. This time, however, he bound the victim's hands and feet with Venetian blind cords and nylon stockings and raped her with a toilet brush handle.

The Masked Rapist was relentless. Over the next seven months, as his attacks escalated, he would abduct women in their cars and break into their houses and apartments through unlocked windows, tying some of them up with nylon cords cut from their Venetian blinds.

In just under three months, he had committed six rapes and 10 attacks. And he was showing no signs of letting up, says former county prosecutor Helen Fahey: "He was a one-person crime wave."

And unfortunately, the general public was largely oblivious of it occurring because the police weren't going out of their way to alert people. They didn't want to cause a public panic.

On October 11, the Masked Rapist forced a 45-year-old woman to drive to a remote location in Arlington, where he raped and robbed her. He had brought a container of Vaseline along with him to use as a lubricant in the attack.

Four days before Christmas 1983, he raped and robbed a 24-year-old Arlington woman after breaking into her apartment through an unlocked window. He brought a dildo with him this time, a sign of the escalating planning that was going into his attacks.

Two weeks into the New Year, on January 14, 1984, a 22-year-old Chinese-American woman returned to the house she was renting with friends and heard noises in her basement. Heading downstairs, she discovered the Masked Rapist, who had broken in via the basement window. He robbed her of her pocketbook at knifepoint, telling her, "All we want is the TV set. If you make a noise, we'll kill the little girl upstairs," apparently referring to one of her roommates, who was sleeping in her bedroom. But as he rifled through her purse, another one of the young woman's roommates was alerted by the noise and descended the basement steps to investigate. Startled, the intruder quickly fled the scene, dropping a small flashlight behind him as he exited the window.

The same night, the rapist stole another woman's purse at knifepoint from her car but before he could do anything else, a bystander stumbled onto the scene, causing the attacker to flee. The rapist had been wearing his homemade mask and a cream-colored, canvas Eisenhower jacket.

Exactly one week later, another woman arrived home to discover evidence of an unsettling break-in. The cords from her Venetian blinds had been cut and were neatly laid out on her bed alongside pornographic books, carrots and other items stolen from her neighbor's house next door.

She got lucky, says retired Arlington homicide detective Joe Horgas: "He found sex paraphernalia [at the neighbor's house] that he brought over and it was on this lady's bed when she came home. Now she got home late that day I think or something, but from the crime scene and everything, it looks like he was there waiting and got tired of waiting for her. But if she got home probably an hour sooner or something, she probably would have been the first."

The first *murder*, that is.

Because only four days later, on January 25, 1984, in the same sleepy, parklike neighborhood, attorney Carolyn Hamm was found bound and strangled to death in the garage of her South 23rd Street home. Hamm lived just a block away from the last two break-ins.

The same day Hamm's body was found, while police were still searching her home for evidence, the Masked Rapist broke into a house six blocks away, carrying out yet another variation of his by-now very familiar M.O.

The 32-year-old homeowner heard a door open downstairs and went to investigate. She found herself face-to-face with the Masked Rapist, who had broken one of the door's window panes and let himself inside. Holding her at knifepoint, he growled, "OK, bitch, where's your purse?"

After grabbing all the cash she had, he carelessly dumped the contents of her purse onto the floor. Then he ordered the terrified woman to disrobe and gave her a dildo, which police would later learn he stole from her next-door neighbor's house. When she refused to use it on herself, the rapist "went crazy" with anger, she later told police. He punched her in the face repeatedly and slashed her across her right calf with the knife, leaving a four-inch scar. He then forced her outside, where he made her perform oral sex on him while holding the knife to her eye.

"There came a point in time when he took her out of the house," Horgas says, relating the woman's story. "They went into the backyard and she doesn't know where they were going. She figured it was going to be to a car or something. But once she gets in the backyard and she's outside, now remember he's got a knife [and] she's outside and she said every animalistic [instinct] that [she] had for survival at that time [came] out and she started screaming. And he kind of sliced [her] up with the knife. She had slashes all over her legs [and] her arms but it saved her life and he ended up jumping over the fence and ran away."

As he fled, the Masked Rapist again dropped a small flashlight.

And with that, as suddenly as the seven months of terrifying attacks had begun, it all came to an abrupt end.

Within two weeks, police arrested David Vasquez, a mentally challenged janitor who worked at a McDonald's restaurant in Manassas, Virginia, and charged him with Hamm's murder. But Horgas had always thought that the African-American Masked Rapist had killed Hamm.

When Carolyn Hamm was murdered, Joe Horgas had been on vacation visiting family back in his Pennsylvania hometown. By the time he returned to work, Vasquez had already been identified as a suspect.

Back then, Horgas explains, the police department's detective divisions were fairly divided. Horgas' unit handled robberies and homicides. But if a robbery included a sexual assault or rape, like the Masked Rapist cases did, it instead went to the sex crimes unit. And while everybody had access to the hot sheet, or logbook of crimes, and they shared information at monthly meetings, the units largely ran their investigations independently of one another.

Horgas was well aware of the Masked Rapist cases, and he was the only one at the time who was asking if there might be a connection between those crimes and the Hamm murder.

But Horgas could sometimes be aggressive and intense, and while his fellow detectives respected him, not everyone liked him.

In author and attorney Paul Mones' 1995 book about the case, *Stalking Justice*, one of Horgas' fellow detectives was quoted as saying, "Joe and I are friends, but he's a hard

Arlington Detective Joe Horgas was the only one who saw a link between the Masked Rapist cases and the murders of Carolyn Hamm and Sue Tucker. (*Photo courtesy Joe Horgas*)

person to work with sometimes. He doesn't think of other people too much when he wants to do something or wants something done; he doesn't think about how the people are feeling or anything like that. It's what he wants _now_ ... and he tends to piss a lot of people off the way he comes across."

Another officer told Mones that "Joe's an abrasive personality. A lot of people don't like Joe; a lot of people like Joe. I don't think there are very many people in between."

None of the other detectives bought into Horgas' theory about a link between the Hamm murder and the Masked Rapist.

"That's a sore subject," Horgas says. "I mean, that was always in the back of my mind. Only it kind of went away after they locked up David Vasquez and everything stopped. So everybody assumes, 'Well, you know, we've got the right guy.' I mean, you understand, everything stopped. Once they locked up Vasquez, _everything stopped._"

However, the other detectives in the department "knew Vasquez wasn't the Masked Rapist because they knew that was a black guy [and] David Vasquez is not black; he's Hispanic."

Eventually, Horgas says, "I told my sergeant, I said, 'Look at the M.O. and look at all this stuff this guy's done and what a coincidence that, within a couple of blocks of Carolyn Hamm's murder, somebody's seen outside the window and it matches [the Masked Rapist's] description and all that.'"

Well, the sergeant told Horgas, if you feel that strongly about it, send out a teletype. So Horgas took his advice and sent a teletype to surrounding jurisdictions to find out if any other departments had arrested anyone matching the Masked Rapist or had any crimes duplicating his M.O.

There was no response.

Essentially, Joe Horgas was like a character from the movies, the hero who's the only one who knows that the aliens are invading or the guy who has evidence that spies have infiltrated the government but no one will listen to him.

"I mean, I worked with all these people," Horgas says, with obvious bewilderment. "I just can't believe that I saw something that they just ignored."

❖

Flash-forward to almost four years later and Joe Horgas was more convinced than ever that not only had the Masked Rapist killed Carolyn Hamm, he had also murdered Sue Tucker.

Horgas pored through all the old case files and the connections between the Tucker and Hamm murders and the Masked Rapist cases seemed as clear as day to him. But that would also create a problem for the department because it would mean that they had wrongly convicted David Vasquez.

And then, on Tuesday, December 8, 1987, a week and a half after Sue Tucker's murder, Horgas would learn that the Masked Rapist had another alias: The South Side Strangler.

"My sergeant had a teletype laying on my desk and it was from Richmond," Horgas says. The document described the identical strangulation murders of Debbie Davis and Dr. Susan Hellams in September and October in the state capital of Richmond, about 100 miles south of Arlington.

The teletype had been sent out by Glenn Williams, who with his partner Ray Williams, was one of the two Richmond homicide detectives investigating the South Side Strangler murders. It read:

FOR POLICE INFORMATION ONLY. NOT FOR PRESS.

THIS DEPARTMENT IS INVESTIGATING TWO HOMICIDES. THE FIRST OCCURRED ON 9-18-87 AROUND MIDNIGHT. A WF-35 WAS FOUND IN HER APARTMENT ON 9-19-87 AT 0940 HOURS. SHE HAD BEEN BOUND WITH HER HANDS TIED BEHIND HER BACK. SHE HAD ALSO BEEN RAPED. THE APARTMENT WAS ENTERED THROUGH AN OPEN REAR WINDOW WITH THE SCREEN CLOSED. THE SUSPECT RAISED THE

SCREEN AND ENTERED THE APARTMENT. THERE WAS NO SIGN OF ANY STRUGGLE IN THE ASSAULT OR THE MURDER.

ON 10-3-87 AT 0140 HOURS THE VICTIM, WF-32, WAS FOUND IN HER BEDROOM. THE HOUSE WAS ENTERED FROM A SECOND STORY WINDOW THAT WAS OPENED BUT THE SCREEN WAS CLOSED. THE SCREEN IN THIS CASE WAS CUT OUT AND LAID ON THE SECOND STORY PORCH.

IN BOTH CASES THE VICTIMS WERE STRANGLED TO DEATH. ANY DEPARTMENT WITH SIMILAR CASE PLEASE CONTACT RICHMOND BUREAU OF POLICE OR DETECTIVE GLENN D. WILLIAMS

THANKS FOR YOUR HELP IN ADVANCE.

As soon as Horgas finished reading the teletype, he called Glenn Williams, who had a few more surprises to share from the Richmond investigation, including the fact that the Strangler was also believed to have killed a 15-year-old high school freshman in Chesterfield County on the weekend before Sue Tucker was murdered.

Additionally, Glenn told Horgas, the Richmond police had sent the semen samples from the South Side Strangler murders up to a private lab in New York for a new process called DNA fingerprinting to see if they could definitively match the killings. Horgas knew virtually nothing about DNA testing except that he had heard it discussed by Arlington prosecutor Helen Fahey as a possibility to be considered in the Tucker murder.

Glenn Williams also told Horgas that FBI profilers believed that the South Side Strangler was a white male in his 20s to 30s.

When Horgas began briefing Glenn about the strangulation murders of Sue Tucker and Carolyn Hamm, Glenn didn't see the connection. Why would the killer strike 100 miles to the north? Besides, the FBI profilers said the Strangler was probably a local Richmond guy.

Horgas then asked if Richmond had reports of any other incidents in the South Side neighborhoods where Debbie Davis and Susan Hellams were murdered.

Glenn replied, "Well, we do have this black guy running around doing some shit."

At 3 a.m. on November 1, he told Horgas, a 33-year-old woman in Westover Hills was startled awake in the bedroom of her first-floor apartment by a black man wearing a ski mask and work gloves. She described the intruder as being in his late 20s with a muscular build. Holding her at knifepoint, he had directed her to disrobe and take a shower. He then forced her to down half a bottle of Southern Comfort whiskey, which he had brought with him in a bag tied to his waist, along with a vibrator and rope, which he used to bind her hands. The attacker raped and assaulted the woman for three hours. Then he started to bind her ankles. The panicked lady's frantic cries drew the attention of her upstairs neighbor, who came downstairs to check on her. The rapist escaped through the kitchen window, taking some of the young woman's accounting textbooks with him, which he dropped as he ran away. The neighbor phoned police, who arrived to find the woman on her bed, bound and gagged.

Horgas was astonished, to say the least. He informed Glenn about Arlington's Masked Rapist cases but Glenn remained skeptical that it could all be the work of the same perpetrator.

Nevertheless, Glenn told Horgas that if he wanted to learn more about the Richmond cases, he could come down and attend their weekly task force meeting the next morning. Horgas immediately secured permission from his sergeant to travel to Richmond with another detective.

And so, Horgas says, "we went down for the meeting the next day and we brought all our pictures and they had all their pictures and we compared it. It didn't take much of a brain to see that everything's done by the same guy.

"Even though it's 100 miles apart, you know, what are the odds that there's a guy killing women [in Richmond] this way and he's killing this woman up in Arlington the same way?"

However, from Joe Horgas' perspective, the Richmond cops initially treated him like a Podunk, small-town detective who lacked their knowledge and breadth of experience.

As he remembers it, "we only had a couple of homicides a year and they had 70 or 80 a year and so, you know, how dare I even put any input into the game."

But retired Richmond homicide detective Ray Williams disputes Horgas' take on the meeting, saying, "That's not true. We made a point not to do that. You don't want to come across as the big-city homicide detective because that would turn him off. ... I never treated him with disrespect."

There's still no love lost between Ray Williams and Joe Horgas. They were both clever, dedicated, successful homicide detectives and this was the biggest case of both of their careers. But they also possess big personalities and egos that clashed. Even 30 years later, they relish taking pot shots at each other. But despite that, they're both in agreement that by the end of that December 1987 meeting, the Richmond task force had accepted that the Arlington murders had probably also been committed by the South Side Strangler.

"We all agreed it was the same person," Ray Williams confirms.

The knowledge that the Strangler was killing women in both Richmond and Arlington made law enforcement realize that the danger was much greater than they'd thought. But knowing that didn't bring detectives in Richmond or Arlington any closer to homing in on a suspect. And so the investigation stalled for another few agonizing weeks while they hoped to catch a break in the case before the Strangler could kill someone else.

On December 29, 1987, Horgas met with Steve Mardigian and Judson Ray, supervisory special agents with the FBI's Behavioral Science Unit, who would establish an updated behavioral profile on the killer, given the new information Horgas had to offer them about the Arlington cases. (Mardigian and Ray were in the unit when actress Jodie Foster visited to prepare for her Academy Award-winning role as an FBI trainee tasked with hunting down the monstrous, skin-wearing serial killer Buffalo Bill in the acclaimed 1992 film *The Silence of the Lambs*.)

In the conference room at his police department Horgas had set up his self-described "traveling show" of displays and diagrams. "We didn't know who the suspect was, but basically I had put together everything that I had to show from the M.O. that whoever was the rapist was the killer," he explains.

Mardigian recalls that he and Ray immediately observed that "there were a lot of behavioral similarities between the Northern Virginia case and the Richmond cases. Boy, we saw some striking similarities there."

Now retired, FBI profiler Steve Mardigian told Horgas that investigating the first Masked Rapist crime would provide key clues for catching the Strangler.

Also now retired, Mardigian says that once Horgas laid out the information from all the cases, it became clear that the 1983, 1984 and 1987 Arlington crimes were also committed by the South Side Strangler.

So, if the Masked Rapist and the South Side Strangler were the same person, then why did the FBI at first suggest that the strangler was likely a white male?

To answer that question, one has to go back to the very origins of the FBI's Behavioral Science Unit, which was co-founded in 1972 by FBI agent Robert Ressler. At the time of the South Side Strangler killings in 1987, it had only been about 10 years since Ressler and his fellow FBI agent John Douglas began their pioneering research into serial killers, interviewing offenders like Edmund Kemper, who had sadistically murdered 10 people, including his own mother and grandparents.

These early prison interviews had one factor in common: All the serial killers that Ressler and Douglas had studied were white.

Mardigian and Ray both say that the first black serial killer the unit was aware of was Wayne Williams, who was convicted in connection with the 1979-1981 Atlanta Child Murders, a case that Judd Ray had worked. At the time of the South Side Strangler murders, it was thought in the unit that serial killing was a phenomenon almost exclusively carried out by white males.

As we now know, that's simply not the case. Serial killers aren't restricted to one race or even gender. Human beings of every race and nationality have the capacity for great acts of kindness, as well as immeasurable cruelty. The amount of melanin in one's skin has nothing to do with whether someone turns out to be a righteous man or a monster. In fact, the two best-known serial killers whose M.O.s have the most in common with the South Side Strangler are the

Louis Schlesinger

Golden State Killer and BTK, both of whom are white.

But in 1987, the FBI's fledgling Behavioral Science Unit had to make its conclusions based on what it knew at the time, says Dr. Louis Schlesinger at the John Jay College of Criminal Justice in New York. "You've got to give a lot of credit to the early folks doing this but you can't hold them to today's standards of 2018 [for] what they were doing in the mid-'70s," Schlesinger says. "As you gain experience, you'll learn. And then you change your methods, change your techniques and we're continuing to learn as well."

The FBI Behavioral Science Unit was composed of about eight agents in 1987 and the prevailing theory at the time was that it was rare for murderers – and especially serial killers – to prey on victims of a different race. Absent any witnesses or physical evidence pointing to the South Side Strangler's race, it was therefore thought that a serial killer murdering white victims would almost certainly be Caucasian.

"We did the same thing with characteristics like age. You go for the norm if you don't have evidence to support another way," Mardigian says, "and you base it on what your prior experience has been." And of course, the FBI had barely been studying the topic for a decade at that point, and only with a small, core group of agents.

"Owing to the lack of forensic evidence to the contrary," he says, "we would have probably deferred at that stage to the intelligence [local police] showed us as [to whether the crime] would have been white-on-white or black-on-black, so to speak, and that's [why] I think [the South Side Strangler] was profiled as a white male in that aspect of it. And of course we wouldn't certainly have said that if we had known there was forensic evidence to the contrary."

Now armed with a far more extensive criminal history for the South Side Strangler, including detailed accounts of his M.O. from rape survivors, the two FBI profilers were now able to provide Horgas with better, more accurate insights into how Arlington and Richmond detectives might catch this serial killer.

"They spent about an hour or two looking over everything and the short story is they ended up agreeing with me that they think this Masked Rapist is the killer," Horgas remembers. "And [then] they said we're going to go one step further: If this first case that you have, the one where he found the woman at the phone booth and made her drive him down to Green Valley, if that's the first case, then he's going to live within a two-block area of where he took her to."

Additionally, Steve Mardigian and Judd Ray concluded that when he was acting as the Masked Rapist, the South Side Strangler wouldn't have stopped raping and killing women of his own volition. Instead, they thought it was far more likely that the Strangler had been jailed for another offense between 1984 and 1987, the period between the murders of Carolyn Hamm and Debbie Davis. It was possible, the FBI agents theorized, that he had recently been paroled to a halfway house.

"We pulled probation [and] parole records looking for anybody that got out of prison that would have lived in that area," Horgas says. "We also asked Richmond to do the same stuff. ... We're looking for someone who got locked up after Carolyn Hamm was killed and who was out prior to [Debbie] Davis being killed down in Richmond."

Joe Horgas asked his fellow officers if they could suggest any suspects from the Green Valley neighborhood who might be their guy. And he also started thinking back to his own days working cases in that area.

"Green Valley was my expertise," he says. "I used to catch all the robberies and everything from down there. It was my forte, I guess. I mean, I was just good with the people down there."

Now called Nauck, the Green Valley community was founded by a free black man, Levi Jones, in 1844. And after the Civil War, the neighborhood became a refuge for newly freed slaves.

One day in December 1987, while Horgas was parking his car in the area near where the first Masked Rapist attack had occurred, a local kid's name popped into his head out of nowhere. Back in 1975 or 1976, Joe had questioned the kid as a juvenile in connection with a break-in complaint from a neighbor but he couldn't recall more than his first name.

"All I could remember was Timmy," Horgas says. "When I first met Timmy, he was probably, I don't know, somewhere around 13, 14 years old. I was working burglaries at the time and I believe he was one of several kids that broke into somebody's house. I know I talked to his mother to get permission to get his fingerprints and I don't remember if we made him by prints or if the kids [snitched] on one another or what, but I know I had to get his fingerprints through the permission of his mom and that's really about the time I met him."

He still doesn't know exactly what it was about the young man that made him think of him. Maybe it was the fact that Timmy had also set fire to his mother's car – just like the Masked Rapist had set one of his victims' cars on fire.

Timmy's family lived just four or five blocks southeast from the site of the first Masked Rapist attack, only about a third of a mile away. He would have been very familiar with the dead end vacant wooded lot where the rapist had taken his first victim. Timmy's home had been just about one mile from homicide victim Carolyn Hamm's house and roughly a mile and a half from the townhouse where Sue Tucker was murdered.

Back at the office, Timmy's full name was on the tip of Joe Horgas' tongue, nagging at the corners of his brain. And as he was sitting at a conference table with another detective poring over an endless stack of parolee records, it came to him: Timmy Spencer.

"We're comparing names against each other and all of a sudden Timmy Spencer's name popped in my head. I finally remembered. And that doesn't mean it's him. It just means it's another one to put into the pile," Horgas says. "But then, when we ran him in the computer and when we found out that he was arrested in Alexandria for a burglary right after Carolyn Hamm was killed, it got our interest."

Horgas discovered Spencer had been arrested in January 1984 for two break-ins in neighboring Alexandria – and he had been wearing the same clothes as the Masked Rapist.

According to the arrest report, Spencer was caught exiting "through a very small rear window, which the suspect had broken out." He had a large amount of stolen collectors' coins in his pockets on his person as well as a knife, a screwdriver and a small flashlight.

"Timmy was seen coming out of one house and going into the other house. Neighbors saw him coming out as he had broken into one house and he was getting ready to go into the other house when they called the police. The police caught him red-handed," Horgas says.

"And so, when you look at the incident report and you see the evidence they had there, I mean, the rapist, he always had something on his hands [and] Timmy's socks were not on his feet. ... He [also] had Puma sneakers on. And in one case on Greenbrier Street, [the Masked Rapist] raped a lady and I think her husband came from work or something in the early stages, maybe in August '83, and [the suspect] escaped by jumping out the bedroom window or bathroom window. But there was a Puma sneaker track left. Well, [Spencer was arrested] wearing Puma sneakers, his socks are not on his feet, they're in his pockets, [and] he's wearing a tan Eisenhower jacket, which is what the rape victims describe the Masked Rapist as wearing. This was all deserving of more looking into."

Horgas next contacted the state probation and parole system to determine Spencer's current location. Spencer, they told Horgas, had been paroled to a halfway house in South Richmond, the Hospitality House, less than a month before the murder of Debbie Davis and he was still living there. It was on the 1500 block of Porter Street, about 1.2 miles (or a 17-minute walk) away from the Hellams murder scene and around 2.4 miles from victim Debbie Davis' apartment.

"And then we go down to Richmond," Horgas says, "and we go to the halfway house and we find out that he signed himself out for every murder down there. And he got a furlough to come up to Arlington for the Susan Tucker murder. So everything just seems to fit the puzzle.

"The pieces are all coming together now."

CHAPTER 6

THE MATCH

It was already past 10 a.m. and lab tech Rena Chapouris was nowhere to be seen at the Medical College of Virginia's Department of Neurosurgery. Nobody knew where she was. And that just wasn't like Rena.

"What happened that morning was Rena didn't show up for work, so it was quite unusual. She was very reliable. She was close to one of the other technicians. She tried to call [Rena] but she wasn't answering her phone," says Rena Chapouris' boss at the time, Ronald Hayes, Ph.D., who was the director of MCV's neurosurgical research labs.

The lab technician who was a close friend of Rena's suddenly became "very distraught," remembers Hayes, "because she had dreams the night before that [Rena] had been killed or something terrible happened to her and she was just rocking back and forth in the chair, just very, very upset."

That morning, Wednesday, January 6, 1988, Hayes and the lab tech left work and picked up Rena's boyfriend of five years, Jim Rushing, a bartender and musician. The three of them took Hayes' car to Rena's Grove Avenue apartment in Richmond's Fan District.

"We went up the stairs to her apartment door and it was ajar, so immediately this was not normal," Hayes says.

Rushing picks the story up from there: "And so we went in and I went to the back bedroom and the place was just a mess, like it's been turned over, like somebody robbed it. And so I went in and I went into the back bedroom and I looked to where the door joined the wall and I could see her body laying on the bed. And then I just told [Hayes], 'I can't go in there,' and he did. I worked at a restaurant about a block away and I just took off downstairs screaming."

"Oh my god! Oh my god!" the panicked young bartender yelled.

"Nobody would go in," Hayes says, "so I went in and saw the apartment living room area in disarray. Obviously [there had] been a scene of some violent disturbance. What I saw was a bloody hammer or something that looked like that on the floor. And then I made myself go inside and I saw [Rena] on the bed and I frankly can't remember what I saw, really. It was not good. So I just sort of stumbled out of the bedroom and we called the police."

The 29-year-old woman was lying face-up on her bed, nude from the waist down. Rena had been strangled with a pink sweater and beaten with a blunt object; her hands were bound together with Venetian blind cords, which were also tied to one of her ankles.

Local news reporters instantly began asking if this was another South Side Strangler murder, even though it had taken place on the north side of the James River in Richmond's Fan District, about three to four miles away from the other slayings.

"I slept basically with a screwdriver in my bed for the first couple of days because I thought it was the South Side Strangler too," Rushing says.

Police would later learn that Rena had worked nights waiting tables part-time at O'Toole's, a popular South Richmond restaurant and pub that South Side Strangler victims Debbie Davis and Dr. Susan Hellams had sometimes patronized.

And like Hellams, Rena had worked at MCV's Department of Neurosurgery and was also found strangled and stripped bottomless.

This MCV connection would set off another panic among Hellams' already grieving and traumatized co-workers. Dr. Lynn Atkinson, one of the last three people to see Susan Hellams alive, says Chapouris' murder created a "total state of paranoia. … It was a very, very scary time and we all were just completely afraid that we might be targeted next because ... he might be targeting residents or people associated with the neurosurgery department at MCV."

Richmond detectives met with neurosurgery employees, Atkinson recalls, and asked if they knew of any aggrieved patients or former employees who might be inclined to pursue a vendetta against MCV.

However, to Richmond homicide detective Ray Williams' trained eye, there were enough differences between the Chapouris and Hellams murder scenes that it was obvious to him at first glance that the Rena Chapouris killing was either a copycat murder or someone trying to disguise it as the work of the South Side Strangler.

For one thing, he says, Rena's hands were bound in front. More importantly, she hadn't been sexually assaulted.

Also, she had been repeatedly beaten in the forehead with a blunt object. Early news reports said it was a hammer, but Williams says it was actually a slapjack – a handheld blackjack-style weapon with a strap. The killer left it behind on the bedroom nightstand, he says. Rena's bed was covered in blood spatter from her head wound and the apartment had been thoroughly ransacked.

"We knew, I knew, within five minutes," remembers Ray. "I said, 'We got a wannabe.'"

Over the years, a lot of rumors have grown up around the Rena Chapouris murder in Richmond, and the case has taken on a mythic quality. Some claim that a cop had been dating Rena and killed her and that the murder was covered up, but Rena's friends and co-workers say she didn't even know any policemen, let alone date any. And no facts have ever emerged to substantiate this rumor or bring it out of the realm of conspiracy theories.

Like a lot of things in life, the real facts in Rena Chapouris' murder seem to be a lot more prosaic.

Hours after Chapouris' body was found, police responded to the suicide of Rena's former roommate, Michael St. Hilaire, about a mile away. A 28-year-old carpenter, St. Hilaire had hanged himself with a wire in the basement of a West Main Street coffeehouse where he had been living with his fiancée, a local artist.

St. Hilaire had struggled with a cocaine addiction for years. Friends said he was self-medicating to deal with the pain from a gunshot wound he had suffered almost a decade earlier, when he was driving an ice cream truck and a robber had shot him in the lower spine.

When Rena Chapouris was found strangled in her Fan District apartment in January 1988, reporters immediately began asking if the South Side Strangler had struck again. (*Photo courtesy Jim Rushing*)

He had also briefly dated Rena's older half-sister and best friend, Mariana Keller.

Mariana says Rena was a spiritual woman who loved her cats and traveling. But Rena was also very trusting and ran with a crowd that included some questionable characters like Michael St. Hilaire. After Mariana broke up with him, St. Hilaire became roommates with Rena for a couple months until Rena kicked him out.

"Rena even called me before that and asked my opinion: 'Do you think it's OK? What do you know about Michael? Is it safe to let him rent a room here?' And this is where I occasionally have some guilt," Mariana says, "because I didn't know the extent of ... Michael had a lot of darkness I didn't understand. I was naive. I know I was naive about people taking drugs, so I did tell her, 'Well, he's kind of a loser in the fact that he cannot be stable and I know he does drugs. But I don't think that would be harmful to you if he pays the rent. That's kind of his separate life.'"

St. Hilaire only ended up staying at Rena's about a month or two. Rena kicked him out of her apartment after accusing him of stealing something from her bedroom.

Police would later definitively declare that St. Hilaire had killed Rena, saying they found matching fibers at the scenes of both Rena's murder and St. Hilaire's suicide. In recent years, there's been some debate about the accuracy of fiber analysis. It's nowhere near as conclusive as DNA testing or even fingerprint identification and is somewhat subjective. Police said that St. Hilaire's motive for killing Rena had been robbery. They cited a journal entry he left behind in which he said he needed money and was about to do something dangerous and might kill himself if he wasn't successful.

Still, even today, not everyone is sure St. Hilaire was really Rena's killer, including her own sister. Mariana says she was told by police that boot prints found on the bed didn't match St. Hilaire's feet.

"Yes, his fingerprints were in the house because he was a roommate there," she says. "That still doesn't prove [anything]. ... In my mind and [among] some of my close friends, we don't really know in our hearts if he did it. We know he was a good scapegoat because he hung himself, which he always threatened to do while he was dating me: 'Oh, Mariana, life sucks. I almost killed myself in your basement today.' *In my basement* – he said he would almost do that. And that's when I kicked him out. I said, 'I'm tired of this crap. You need to go fix yourself and not be telling me that.'"

One thing was clear, though: No matter who killed Rena Chapouris, the sight of yet another young woman ruthlessly strangled to death had left Richmond homicide detective Glenn Williams depressed and dispirited. More than three months after the murder of Debbie Davis, he and his partner Ray still weren't any closer to catching the South Side Strangler and Glenn had had enough.

By this point, concerned groups and individuals had put up almost $50,000 in reward money for information leading to the arrest and conviction of the South Side Strangler, but it had all amounted to nothing.

Sitting in their unmarked car outside the latest murder scene, Glenn sighed, telling Ray, "You know, this is frustrating."

"Glenn, we work hard. We'll get a break," Ray reassured his partner. "You make your own breaks in this thing. Just stay with me. We'll get it done."

But Glenn only "got more distant," Ray remembers. "He sat in the car, wouldn't say anything for an hour at a time. You have to be careful around cops that are quiet because they are internalizing a lot of this stuff."

The break in the case the Williams Boys had been looking for would come far sooner than they knew, however.

Later that evening, the same day that Rena Chapouris' body was found, Ray and Glenn received a call from Arlington homicide detective Joe Horgas, who said he knew who the South Side Strangler was: A recent parolee from Arlington named Timothy Wilson Spencer.

Detective Joe Horgas

Bullshit, Glenn replied.

Spencer had been jailed for breaking and entering into houses just after the 1984 murder of Carolyn Hamm in Arlington, Horgas related to his Richmond counterparts, and what's more, Spencer had been released to a halfway house for parolees in South Richmond just *two weeks* before the murder of Debbie Davis. Horgas told them that he had personally confirmed that Spencer had checked out of the halfway house during each of the murders and had obtained a furlough to travel home to Arlington for Thanksgiving weekend, when Sue Tucker was killed.

The next morning, Horgas met the Williams Boys and their lieutenant for breakfast at a hotel restaurant in Fredericksburg, the halfway point along the north-south Interstate 95 between Richmond and Arlington. Once again, Horgas laid out his findings for the Richmond detectives, bringing them up to speed on his part of the investigation.

Glenn Williams was doubtful that Horgas had cracked the case. Ray Williams was open to the idea that Spencer could be the Strangler, but to this day, he remains skeptical that Horgas just came up with Spencer's name out of thin air after he remembered questioning him as a juvenile. He thinks that Horgas must have just come across Spencer by sheer luck while digging through parolee records and Williams maintains that he would have eventually come across it too. Former Arlington prosecutor Helen Fahey, however, corroborates Horgas' account, saying he has never wavered from it and, what's more, Horgas told her that's how it happened right after he came up with Spencer's name.

Because Horgas didn't have any direct evidence like fingerprints or witnesses linking Spencer to the crime scenes, Horgas' commanding officer and Fahey wouldn't approve an arrest. But Spencer was scheduled to travel back to Arlington that coming weekend and Horgas needed the Richmond police to coordinate surveillance with him. If they could catch Spencer in the act of breaking into a house or doing something else illegal, they could at least take him into custody.

That prospect, however, made Fahey exceedingly nervous. What if police lost sight of Spencer? What if he broke into a house and killed someone before they could arrest him?

"Surveillance always sounds much better in the books than it does in real life. To actually do a full surveillance of anyone takes a tremendous number of people and it's still very, very difficult," explains Fahey. "And I said, 'Once he gets away, suppose he gets away, suppose you lose him and tomorrow morning you find out that some other woman was murdered half a block away?'"

Serial sexual murderers like the South Side Strangler possess a compulsion to kill, explains Louis Schlesinger, Ph.D., an expert on serial killers and professor of forensic psychology at the John Jay College of Criminal Justice in New York.

"The best way to understand serial sexual murder is to see it as an abnormal sexual arousal pattern," Schlesinger says. "These people are not killing just because it's fun to do that and they want to do it. It's exceptionally arousing for them sexually. In these individuals there's a fusion of sex and aggression so that the aggressive act itself is eroticized and ... that's the main motivation for them."

The South Side Strangler took "sexual gratification from inflicting pain on others" but also experienced a perverse pleasure from dominating his victims, the professor points out.

"The offender knows he is in complete control of the victim and that's what's most arousing," says Schlesinger. "It's not just inflicting pain; it's controlling the person. So when he would strangle somebody, as they were about to die, he would release the ligature so that they could come to and then continue the strangling and in that way prolong the sadistic aggression and that is what [was] sexually arousing to him."

Fahey and Horgas "managed to get the Richmond Police *somewhat* interested in [performing] some surveillance down there [on Spencer]," Fahey says, "but they didn't want to do it because they didn't think it was the guy."

Due to an unexpected snowstorm, Spencer ended up not traveling to Arlington and the Richmond officers reluctantly began their surveillance.

Timothy Spencer had been under surveillance for just a few days when he was pulled over by a Richmond squad car while driving a borrowed car with two female passengers inside – a local woman Spencer was dating and her best friend. The two women had been suspected of shoplifting from Cloverleaf Mall and a nearby supermarket.

Ray Williams radioed the patrolman who pulled over Spencer and told him to let Spencer and his friends go with a warning, even though driving a car was a clear violation of Spencer's parole. They needed to catch Spencer in the act of doing something a whole lot more incriminating than driving, however.

After the squad car pulled away, the undercover officers who had been tailing Spencer witnessed him doing something curious: He crawled under the car, sprawled on his back in three inches of snow, searching the vehicle's undercarriage.

"He checked it every night," says Williams, adding that Spencer never found the radio tracker that police installed on the car. In Ray Williams' 30-year career, he never heard about another suspect searching for a tracker on their vehicle while they were under surveillance.

While under surveillance by Richmond Police in January 1988, Spencer was observed hanging around Cloverleaf Mall and spending the night with a girlfriend.

Plainclothes Richmond police officers also observed Spencer committing parole violations like spending the night at his girlfriend's house. This was despite the fact that he was supposed to be living at the halfway house as a condition of his parole. Spencer was also seen hanging out for hours at a time at Cloverleaf mall, which had strong links to all three Richmond-area Strangler victims, as well as another popular local indoor mall, Chesterfield Towne Center, located about five miles west on Midlothian Turnpike in a more affluent, suburban area of the county. It was an intriguing clue, Ray Williams says, but police never spotted Timothy Spencer do anything overtly incriminating. And after two weeks of not being able to directly connect him to the South Side Strangler killings, Ray told a horrified Helen Fahey and Joe Horgas that Richmond was pulling its surveillance of Spencer.

Ray maintains that's because Spencer was clearly aware of the surveillance and had altered his behavior patterns. For instance, he says, Spencer would no longer walk down alleys and instead stuck to main streets.

But Fahey and Horgas say they were told that the Richmond brass said that the surveillance was taking too much manpower and there were no signs that Spencer was the killer.

"So they watch him. … They surveil him … and they let us know we don't think this is the right guy, so we're dropping the surveillance. Well, Helen panicked and we had a big meeting," Horgas recalls.

As an elected office holder, Arlington County Commonwealth's Attorney Helen Fahey knew that it could be seriously embarrassing to her if they arrested Spencer and couldn't prove he committed the crimes – or worse yet, if Spencer turned out not to be the killer after all. But wasn't the public safety more important than any risk to her political career?

At this point, the retired Arlington prosecutor says, it was more than apparent that they needed to cross the Rubicon.

"The choice," Fahey says, "was do you take the chance on leaving someone you believe is a serial murderer on the street? It appears that Timothy Spencer is a very, very dangerous serial murderer rapist and from the time that he got out of the penitentiary in '87, in a little over two months, he had murdered and raped three women and one teenage girl. And looking at that, it was pretty clear that as long as he was out there, there were going to be more of these murders."

So Fahey and Horgas did the only thing they could: Assembling all the information they had compiled on Spencer, Fahey presented their case to the Arlington County Grand Jury, which on Wednesday, January 20, 1988, returned indictments against Timothy Spencer for rape, murder and burglary in the strangulation bondage killing of Sue Tucker.

Horgas called the shocked Williams Boys to tell them to get ready because he was coming down to Richmond to take Timothy Spencer into custody.

But before he drove to Richmond, Horgas stopped at Timothy Spencer's mother's home in Arlington's Green Valley neighborhood. Her modest house was located within blocks of the site of the first Masked Rapist attack and about a 20-minute walk from murder victim Sue Tucker's Fairlington Villages townhome.

Speaking with Spencer's mother and grandmother, Horgas told them he wanted to search their home for stolen goods in connection with a break-in over Thanksgiving weekend. The suspect's mother told Horgas that she couldn't remember if Timothy had been home for Thanksgiving but he definitely came home for Christmas because he had given her a gift of some glassware. She had insisted on getting a receipt from Timothy, she told Horgas sadly, because she wanted to ensure that the gift hadn't been stolen. Horgas searched her house but didn't find anything connected to the Arlington crimes.

Later that afternoon, Horgas, the Williams boys and a large team of plainclothes officers assembled outside the Hospitality House on the 1500 block of Porter Street in South Richmond. The halfway house for paroled felons was two miles from the apartment where Debbie Davis had been strangled to death and barely a mile from Susan Hellams' house. Both murder sites were easy walks via main roads.

They were waiting for Spencer to return from his blue-collar job at The Pine Factory, a furniture manufacturer and retailer in Ashland, Virginia, about a 20-minute drive away in Hanover County. They knew he was due back to the halfway house for a mandatory house meeting at around 6 p.m.

When Timothy Spencer pulled up in a borrowed brown Chevrolet sedan at around 10 minutes to 6, he had no idea he was surrounded.

"I don't even know how many people were involved, but I know we were outside the halfway house waiting for him to come home," Horgas remembers. "And when he comes home, short story is he walks into the halfway house and about the same time he's checking in, we're there to arrest him. I didn't tell him he was under arrest for murder. I told him he was under arrest for burglary because burglary was one of the indictments."

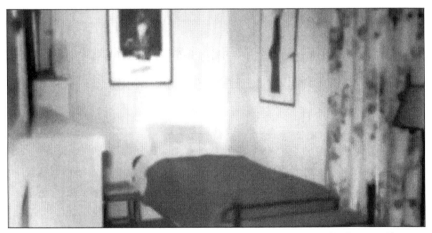

Timothy Spencer's room at the halfway house shortly before police began searching it on January 20, 1988. They would find the words "I hope" scrawled above a figure 8 on the bed's box springs.

A light-skinned, handsome, young African-American man, Spencer had striking hazel eyes and short, close-cropped hair with a neatly trimmed mustache. He was average height, maybe even a little short, and on the thin side but athletic-looking. Far from appearing evil or menacing, he was quiet and acted somewhat stupefied.

Presented with the arrest warrant in the entrance foyer of the halfway house, Spencer was told his bond was $250,000.

"For a burglary? Isn't that kind of high?" Spencer asked in astonishment, glancing around at all the policemen who'd been sent to arrest him.

"Geez, I don't know why the judge did that," Horgas claimed innocently.

Spencer signed a form advising him of his constitutional rights and gave his consent for the police to search his belongings.

Inspecting Spencer's bedroom in the halfway house, Horgas and the other officers found a wool stocking cap and a pair of winter gloves. They also discovered two, long, sturdy screwdrivers, the type favored by burglars for breaking into houses. There was more contraband, as well: a folding hunting knife and a box of .25 caliber ammo. The possession of either item was a definite parole violation.

Police found no stolen objects from the murder scenes, however.

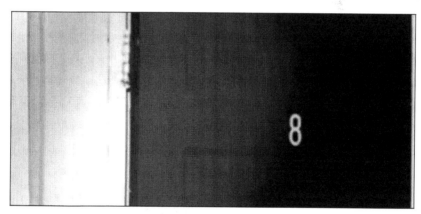

From September 1987 to January 1988, Timothy Spencer lived in Room No. 8 at the Hospitality House halfway house on Porter Street in South Richmond.

Ray Williams believes that Spencer stored his "murder kit" with his mask and any "trophies" taken from the murders in a hidden location probably not far from the halfway house. Someone may have found the items at some point, not realizing their significance, he says. Or, they may still be squirreled away somewhere even today.

Ray remembers finding a bottle of red nail polish that he believed to be the same nail polish that had been used to paint the figure 8 on Diane Cho's thigh, but Horgas and others don't recall this happening and it was not introduced into evidence at Spencer's eventual trial for Cho's murder.

When Ray flipped over the mattress in Spencer's room, Horgas spied something on the fabric covering the box springs: a large, roughly drawn figure 8 with the words "I hope" scrawled above it in magic marker.

Joe called Glenn over and asked if it looked to him like the same symbol that had been painted on Diane Cho's body.

"Jesus! Seems like it," Glenn replied.

Asked if he had drawn it, Spencer nonchalantly answered that he'd never seen it before.

Spencer's bedroom in the halfway house was Room No. 8.

In the car on the return trip to Arlington, Horgas sat in the back seat of an unmarked police car with the handcuffed Spencer. They chatted about Spencer's old neighborhood, his childhood and how Horgas had met when him when he was a teen.

After about 30 minutes, Horgas told Spencer that they were going to need to get a blood sample from him.

Pausing for a second, Spencer asked, "Does this involve a rape?"

"Rape? What makes you say rape?" Horgas asked. "Your charge is burglary."

"Well, you only want blood if there's a rape," Spencer responded.

"No," Horgas told him. "A lot of burglars cut themselves when they break windows."

Spencer's retort? "Well, I didn't cut myself."

"He knew he didn't cut himself," Horgas explains, "so that's why he didn't hesitate on giving his blood."

Spencer then asked Horgas where the burglary he was being arrested for occurred.

Fairlington Villages, Horgas told him.

"Does this have anything to do with the murder?" Spencer asked.

"Why are you asking about that?" Horgas said.

"I live close to Fairlington," Spencer replied, unfazed. "I read the papers and everything. I know what's going on up there."

When they returned to Arlington, police obtained a sample of Spencer's blood and Horgas began interrogating Spencer. The FBI profilers told Horgas that he should begin by attempting to get Spencer to confess to burglary because serial killers seldom confess to murders right away. But Spencer had already figured out that he was suspected for Sue Tucker's murder and despite Joe Horgas' best efforts, he wouldn't admit to anything.

When Horgas told Spencer that he had slipped up by leaving his sperm at the murder scene, Spencer shot back, "Well, you ain't *got* my sperm."

"He was kind of smug," Horgas remembers. "I mean, believe me, I worked on him. I mean, [in] most of my cases I get confessions. [But] I didn't get one in this case. Richmond came up and they worked on him a couple of days later."

Over 12 hours of interviews, the Williams Boys didn't get much farther with Spencer, but Ray Williams proudly notes that he *was* able to get Spencer, who had frequently borrowed an automatic transmission car from a halfway house employee, to acknowledge that he didn't know how to drive a stick-shift. That fact was extremely relevant, given that the

Spencer was interrogated in Arlington following his January 1988 arrest.

South Side Strangler had abandoned victim Debbie Davis' manual-transmission Renault Alliance just blocks from her apartment, with the engine still running.

The only time Spencer seemed rattled was when detectives showed him photos of Sue Tucker's hideously decomposed corpse. At that moment, Spencer appeared fully aware of the seriousness of his predicament and blurted out, "I didn't do this! This is bad, real bad. I know somebody's out to get my ass if they say I did some shit like that. You're all looking at me like I have two sides. Like I'm some kind of Jack the Ripper or Dr. Jekyll and Mr. Hyde. Like I turn into a mutant killer or something like that. There ain't nothing wrong with me. I had nothing to do with this murder."

"I mean, he just denied everything. There was no getting through to him," Horgas says.

Some of that may have been due to the fact that even though he was only 25 years old, Spencer was a savvy, hardened criminal who had spent his teen years in and out of juvenile correctional centers and, as an adult he'd already served three stretches in prison for burglaries.

Another explanation for Spencer's reticence to talk may have been cultural, according to retired FBI profiler Judd Ray, who is himself African-American: "Growing up in the South, black boys are sometimes taught not to be verbal talking to white people, whether the cops or whatever. It's not that they're trying to hide anything; it's just [their] socialization."

With Spencer in custody and a sample of his blood now obtained, it was just a matter of playing the waiting game. Lacking witnesses, fingerprints or any other direct evidence, there was only one way they were going to be able to prove that Timothy Spencer was the South Side Strangler – through a brand-new forensic science method called DNA fingerprinting.

"The whole idea of DNA was just sort of starting to percolate and none of us knew much about it," Fahey says, "but we finally focused in on the fact that if we could get a sample from Spencer and his

DNA matched the crime scenes, then we'd have good, solid evidence."

Back in fall 1987, after the murders of Debbie Davis and Dr. Susan Hellams, a private DNA testing lab in New York called Lifecodes had approached Dr. Paul Ferrara, the director of Virginia's state forensic science lab.

At that time, DNA testing was a new technology less than 10 years old and it had primarily been used for paternity testing. But DNA fingerprinting had also been utilized successfully in a murder case in Europe and a U.S. rape trial in Florida, so Lifecodes was now eager to prove to Virginia that they could use it to solve even tougher cases such as the South Side Strangler serial killings. As one of the nation's leading forensic scientists, Ferrara fully understood the possibilities that DNA testing offered and immediately took Lifecodes up on its offer to help.

Richmond Police sent semen samples collected at the Davis and Hellams murder scenes to Lifecodes for analysis and the lab confirmed in December 1987 that Debbie Davis and Dr. Susan Hellams had both been killed by the same then-unknown man.

In late December 1987 Joe Horgas personally flew to Lifecodes' New York state headquarters to hand-deliver semen samples collected from the murders of Carolyn Hamm and Sue Tucker as well as two of the 1983 rapes. (There were only three evidence kits remaining from the Masked Rapist attacks; the police department's evidence division had already destroyed the rest.)

Horgas returned to Lifecodes in late January to deliver samples of Timothy Spencer's blood.

In those early days of DNA analysis, it could take anywhere from six to 10 weeks to get the results back – and that was on the quick side.

One of the case's investigators would never find out if Spencer's DNA had been a match, however.

By early February 1988, Richmond homicide detective Glenn Williams was becoming increasingly withdrawn and Ray Williams knew something was seriously wrong with his partner.

"He was real distant with me," Ray recalls.

On the afternoon of February 3, Glenn was sitting at his desk, and said, "I'm going out."

"I'll ride with you," Ray offered.

"Nobody will ride with me ever again," Glenn said, leaving the office.

Ray went to their sergeant and told him that Glenn was in trouble and the commanding officer tried to speak with Glenn, but he wouldn't talk about what was bothering him.

That night, Richmond Police Major V. Stuart Cook, who would later serve for 20 years as the elected sheriff of nearby Hanover County, radioed Ray Williams, who was at Cloverleaf Mall, and said he needed Ray to meet with him. Cook told Ray to stay put; he would be there soon.

"It was 9 or 10 o'clock at night. I said, 'Uh-oh, wonder what I did,'" Ray remembers. "We met [and Cook] says, 'Glenn just shot himself. He's dead.'"

Cook asked Ray to drive him to Glenn's suburban Chesterfield County home, about five miles west of Cloverleaf Mall. However, Chesterfield officers had to come to the mall to help them get there, remembers Ray, "Because my mind shut down. I couldn't tell you how to get to Glenn's house. I'd probably been there 30 times."

What Glenn hadn't been telling Ray or anyone else was that at the same time that Ray and Glenn were getting more and more frustrated by their lack of progress on the South Side Strangler case, Glenn's marriage had been falling apart. Glenn shot himself in the chest at point-blank range with his own 9mm handgun shortly after arguing with his wife in their bedroom. He was 38 years old.

The Williams Boys' partnership had come to an end.

"He was lying in bed and watching *Hee-Haw* on TV and they got into this argument, whatever, and he walked over, got the gun from the drawer, put it through his heart and *Boom!*" Ray says, sorrowfully. "He internalized a lot of stuff. ... Cops are famous for killing themselves. Now, Glenn had dated his wife since high school and I'm sure that was a contributing factor but [the Strangler case also] really got on Glenn's nerves. ... Probably the last two weeks before he killed himself, [he was] very distant. Looking into his eyes was like looking into emptiness."

Ray Williams says his partner, Glenn, was becoming increasingly withdrawn as the South Side Strangler case dragged on. "Looking into his eyes was like looking into emptiness," he remembers. (*Photo by Scott Elmquist*)

Local TV news channels reported that city homicide detective Williams committed suicide, Ray Williams says. "Well, my ex-wife and two daughters heard it on the TV and called me and said, 'What's this suicide?' And I said, 'Glenn.' 'Oh,' she said. 'I knew it wouldn't be you. You're too damn stubborn.'"

Glenn Williams, Ray says, "was a great guy."

Cook was quoted in the *Richmond Times-Dispatch* saying that Glenn "was one of the most energetic and dedicated investigators we had. With all the tragedy he saw, experienced and investigated, he never lost his sensitivity toward his victims. He never allowed the job to harden him."

Glenn's suicide surprised everyone who had met him during the South Side Strangler investigation.

Ronald Hayes says he never saw any sign of anything wrong with Glenn when he was investigating the murder of Rena Chapouris just weeks before: "It was just one more shock in what seemed to be an ever-constricting circle of death that surrounded the assault. Now, you know, these were even more innocent times. This was unprecedented. This wasn't an age when high school students were offing each other every week. This was a different age."

In the aftermath of Glenn's suicide, Ray Williams mourned his partner but he also kept working the investigation, trying to bolster the case against Spencer.

Ray eventually tracked down both Spencer's former girlfriend and her best friend. When he and Chesterfield Detective Ernest Hazzard showed up at the best friend's South Richmond house, she casually informed them that she was in the process of burning some of Spencer's letters to the girlfriend in a 55-gallon drum in her backyard.

"I grabbed the letters out before they burned. If it had been two minutes later, they would have burned," Ray recalls. "Ernie said, 'Boy, that was *luck*!' [A] good buddy told me you make your own luck. You hustle, do things right and you make your own luck."

The best friend had wanted to burn the letters to protect her friend from getting dragged into the murder investigation. As it turns out, Spencer had been writing and calling his ex-girlfriend in an effort to get her to provide him with an alibi for the murders. The ex-girlfriend's best friend had never liked Spencer and told Ray Williams she thought there was something dangerous about him.

Singed around the edges, Spencer's letters were still totally legible. Rife with misspellings and grammatical errors, one missive from

Spencer read:

"How's live been treating you! Well I know one thing, its treating you better than me. But babie I'm hanging in there. ... I fill a hole lot better knowing that youre willing to come to court for me. ... Your a lifesaver cause this is some shit, the way that they are trying to put this on me. And its not that I'm telling you to come and lie for me. Because you know for yourself that I was over your house on the nights them people got killed. ... Please help me and come to court and tell these people wear the fuck I was at. Love you, Tim."

When Williams interviewed the ex-girlfriend, she denied that she had been with Spencer on the nights of the murders and she agreed to allow police to monitor her communications with him.

She wrote Spencer back, replying, "Why are you saying I can help you out? You need my help for what[?] Please tell me why. Tim, I'm getting along with my life. Tim, why are you saying you was with me when you wasn't[?] Tim are you telling me to lie for you[?] Cause I would like to know."

In his final letter to her, Spencer responded, "I'm not asking for you to lie for me. Believe me ... I never do that to you, or to anyone. ... Please help me get out of here. Please ... help me out. ... its wrong what these police are doing to me. ... Please keep in touch with me ... I need your help!"

Meanwhile, Arlington Detective Joe Horgas had been calling Lifecodes almost every day to see if there was anything new to report on the DNA results.

On Wednesday, March 16, 1988, there was.

"I'll never forget when we did the testing on these two purportedly unrelated cases [and] we came up with the same DNA profile," says geneticist Michael Baird, Ph.D., who was the director of Lifecodes.

Lifecodes forensic scientist Lisa Bennett called Horgas with the news that Spencer's DNA had been matched to DNA from the Arlington and Richmond crimes.

Timothy Spencer was the South Side Strangler.

"The first person I went to was Helen Fahey to let her know it was a match. I got a kiss [on the cheek] from her," recalls Horgas, laughing heartily at the memory.

Lifecodes had matched Timothy Spencer's DNA to DNA collected from semen on a blue sleeping bag and a pink nightgown at the Sue Tucker murder scene. Lifecodes also matched Spencer's DNA to semen samples from the murders of Debbie Davis and Susan Hellams, as well as semen from one of the 1983 Masked Rapist attacks and the fall 1987 bondage rape of a South Richmond woman. The only bad piece of news was that Lifecodes was unable to extract DNA from a semen-stained robe found at the Carolyn Hamm murder site. The sample was too degraded and recovering DNA from it was beyond the limits of the technology at that time.

Lifecodes scientists calculated the odds of two unrelated African-American males sharing the same sequences of genetic markers at one in 135 million. At the time, the entire African-American population of the United States – men, women and children – numbered only about 29 million.

It was a milestone for both forensic science and American law enforcement, says Lawrence Kobilinsky, Ph.D, a biology professor at the John Jay College of Criminal Justice in New York and an expert on DNA analysis and forensic science.

"This was the first killing that was solved through DNA analysis, so it's a very important case in the history of DNA," Kobilinsky says.

"It really established the fact that DNA was a useful tool for connecting a suspect to a particular crime," says Kenneth E. Melson, former acting director of the federal Bureau of Alcohol, Tobacco, Firearms and Explosives (ATF). A past president of the American Academy of Forensic Sciences, Melson teaches courses on forensic science at the George Washington University Law School and is very familiar with the South Side Strangler case.

"That really set the stage for the use of DNA around the country, not only for pinpointing suspects or defendants in a particular case and connecting them to the crime, but it established other precedents as well," Melson says. "What that did was really catapult DNA into the forensic field in law enforcement. So it was a tremendous advancement in forensic science."

For Arlington prosecutor Helen Fahey, though, the historic DNA match was just the beginning. She would still need to convince 12 jurors that this new DNA science that they'd never even heard of was accurate enough to convict a man for capital murder – in a case without any fingerprints, witnesses or other physical evidence connecting Timothy Spencer to the crime scene.

"The whole trial came down to whether or not the jury would accept the DNA as evidence," Fahey says, "because if they didn't, they were going to acquit him because they had no other evidence to rely on."

CHAPTER 7

THE TRIALS

When people who were there look back on Timothy Spencer's landmark July 1988 capital murder trial for the bondage rape and killing of Sue Tucker, they recall one moment in particular – and it didn't have anything to do with DNA or the veritable army of scientists with impressive credentials who were brought in to testify.

For most of the trial, the accused South Side Strangler was disengaged, seemingly emotionless and disinterested as he sat at the defense table, wearing a pink pin-stripe shirt with a burgundy tie and gray slacks. But as crime-scene photos of Sue Tucker's nude, horrifically decomposed body were being admitted into evidence, Timothy Spencer perked up, onlookers say.

"The only time I really saw him show emotion was when Helen [Fahey] was showing the pictures to the jury. He craned his neck to look at the pictures. He made a real effort," recalls Carl Womack, one of Spencer's two defense attorneys in the Arlington County trial.

"Everyone in the courtroom noticed it. You couldn't *not* notice it. And I was just upset. I was like, 'Tim, this is not a good career move for you. You do not want to be doing what you're doing.'"

Retired Arlington County prosecutor Helen Fahey says that Spencer "really didn't show much reaction to anything when I was cross-examining him, but he seemed to have more interest in the pictures than he had in much of the rest of the proceedings."

During the jury selection, Womack's fellow defense attorney on the case, Thomas J. Kelley Jr. (now an Arlington County judge), had described the photos of Tucker as "personally offensive or gruesome. ... To say that they're not very nice pictures is an understatement."

At the trial's closing, in the sentencing phase, the last witness on the stand would be Spencer himself. His defense attorneys asked him softball questions about his upbringing and childhood misdeeds such as when he got suspended for being one of a group of boys who were playing with firecrackers and set a roll of toilet paper ablaze in an elementary school bathroom.

"Whoever did those crimes was not a good person [and] didn't deserve to walk on the face of the earth with free people anymore," says Carl Womack, Spencer's lead defense attorney for his Arlington capital murder trial.

When Carl Womack asked Spencer if he was guilty, Spencer replied, "I didn't kill those ladies and I feel sorry for their families. I *never* killed those ladies and I ask you not to sentence me to death."

Then it was Helen Fahey's turn. On cross-examination, the Arlington prosecutor just had three questions for Timothy Spencer:

"I show you Commonwealth's Exhibit 2-P. Did you get a good look at that picture earlier?" she asked.

"Yes, I did," Spencer responded about the photo of Sue Tucker's corpse.

She asked him the exact same question about two other crime-scene photos, this time of the bodies of South Side Strangler victims

Debbie Davis and Dr. Susan Hellams: Did you get a good look at that picture?

"Yes I did," Spencer answered twice more.

A few minutes later, when it came time to argue to the jury that Timothy Spencer deserved the death penalty, Helen Fahey mentioned the photos once again:

Arlington County Commonwealth's Attorney Helen Fahey, circa 1980s (*Photo courtesy Helen Fahey*)

"I would suggest," she told the jury, "that you think about Spencer's demeanor and his conduct

during the course of this trial. None of you, *none of us* in this courtroom can look at those pictures without sorrow, without a certain horror, without revulsion.

"If you will recall when Officer Schoembs stood in front of you and showed you the pictures of Susan Tucker, did the defendant look away? No. He wanted to get a good look at those pictures. He wanted to get a good look at those pictures because he wanted to see what it looked like, what *Susan Tucker* looked like, what his *handiwork* looked like, three or four days later."

The prosecutor summed up her argument, telling the jurors, "He also looked at the pictures of Debbie Davis. He looked at the pictures of Susan Hellams. None of us will ever understand why. Something is terribly, terribly wrong with Timothy Spencer."

Fahey rested her case.

"She almost did not need to say anything else," Womack says. "She did a really good job."

It would be the first – and arguably most important – of the four, back-to-back capital murder trials that Timothy Spencer, the accused South Side Strangler serial killer, would face over the next year.

In addition to TV, newspaper and magazine reporters, the courtroom gallery was also filled with the defense attorneys and prosecutors who would be arguing Spencer's three Richmond-area capital murder trials. All of them were there to see if the jury would deliver a conviction based on DNA evidence.

As WRVA 1140 AM News Radio reported, "This is the first case in Virginia where genetic fingerprinting is being used to try to prove the case against an accused serial killer, Timothy Spencer. It may be the first time it's [been] used in the nation. Scientists showed the jury slides so that they could see for themselves if genes from Spencer's blood match genes from semen stains found at the murder scene."

Make no mistake, however: People were also there to grab a peek at Timothy Spencer – to see firsthand what a monster looks like in person. Many of them were probably a little disappointed.

"I think you have this idea that you would recognize someone as evil if you saw them and he was just an ordinary person," Fahey says. "He didn't really react to anything. He didn't look angry. He didn't look really *anything*."

"I'm pretty good at making people laugh and getting them to joke with me," says retired defense attorney Carl Womack. In the entire year he represented Spencer, Womack only saw him laugh once: "It was during the trial and one of the three chairs at the counsel table had a cushion and I'm the eldest and Tim sat in that chair. I said, 'Tim, get up. That's for me.' And he said, 'Yeah, you are pretty old.'"

The six-day trial depended almost entirely on DNA.

As Fahey informed the jury in her opening statements, "There are no eyewitnesses in this case. You don't have eyewitnesses in situations like this. But you will have in this case evidence [that] perhaps is even better than an eyewitness because the defendant left something of himself behind at the murder scene."

Aside from the DNA, the only pieces of physical evidence connecting Timothy Spencer to Sue Tucker's murder were pubic hairs found at the murder scene and a shard of broken glass recovered from Spencer's camouflage jacket. Lab techs found the glass when processing Spencer's belongings that police had collected from the halfway house in Richmond and an expert testified that the fragments matched the glass from the laundry room window the killer had broken at Sue Tucker's townhome. (Another forensic expert said that the pubic hairs recovered were microscopically consistent with Spencer's hair but this sort of visual comparison analysis of hair is almost universally considered outdated and inaccurate now. DNA technology at the time was not sophisticated enough to extract DNA from the hair.)

Helen Fahey's secret weapon in court was her deputy prosecutor, Arthur Karp. Unlike the average lawyer, Art Karp held a bachelor's degree in physics and a master's in mathematics. He had been a systems analyst for the Navy for 20 years before he changed careers and got his law degree. He was a principled death penalty opponent and had protested the Vietnam War. He was also the type of guy who read science books for fun and he was thrilled to be working on a trial that a lot of courtroom observers would later describe as being not unlike sitting through a really heavy university science lecture.

"What the case hinged on really was it was sort of a battle of the experts," Karp says, "keeping in mind that not only was the use of DNA very new but it was very controversial. So the real problem from my point of view was, how do I go about convincing a jury that they should convict somebody of murder, just on the basis of this technical thing that they had never heard anything about before?"

As he sought experts to deliver testimony in the case, Karp started at the top – calling Dr. James Watson, the Nobel Prize-winning molecular biologist who co-discovered the structure of DNA in 1953. Watson wasn't available to testify, he told Karp, but he discussed the case with him and helped connect Karp with other expert witnesses.

"Yeah, that was exciting, I tell you," Karp says. "I still brag about that."

Womack, who was good friends with Art Karp, knew that arguing against the DNA test results was going to be extremely challenging – to say the least.

"The only really bad day I had in the whole case was the day I saw DNA come in as a match for [Spencer] because I figured it was going to be credible. I figured it was going to be admissible," Womack says. "At the pretrial hearing [co-counsel] Tom [Kelley] and I even offered to concede. And I tried to blame it on [Spencer's] blood relatives. [I] almost got away with it."

The only people who have the exact same DNA are identical twins. Other than that, parents and their children share some matching DNA fragments. Womack tried to bring this up, claiming that perhaps a familial connection could create a false positive result. But a DNA expert didn't agree and Karp defused the argument with a wry objection to the judge, noting that Timothy Spencer's mother wasn't a suspect in the murder.

The objection was sustained.

For good measure, Art Karp then asked to approach the bench. Out of earshot of the jury, Karp threatened to bring on the evidence of the DNA matches from the Richmond murders to prove that Timothy Spencer committed the crimes, and not any of his relatives. Faced with the prospect of jurors possibly learning for the first time that his client was also an accused *serial killer*, Carl Womack quickly agreed to back down from that argument. (The Richmond killings would not be brought up to jurors until the sentencing phase of the trial, after the jury had already rendered their verdict against Spencer.)

Womack also vigorously, but unsuccessfully, tried to poke holes in the handling of the physical evidence. The police and lab technicians had impeccably documented the chain of custody for the collection and testing of the semen-stained nightgown and sleeping bag collected at the Sue Tucker murder scene.

Later in the trial, Sue Tucker's widower, Reg Tucker, took the stand, sorrowfully telling his story of being overseas and calling home again and again and getting no answer until a homicide detective finally picked up the phone.

"It was hard because Spencer laughed at me. I could see him looking at me and kind of snickering," Reg remembers. "And his family was really nasty to me, kind of staring me down. I felt like I was on trial."

Being in the same room with Spencer, the man accused of raping and murdering his wife, was tough enough, Reg says, but he was even more shocked at the realization that he *recognized* Spencer.

Upon seeing the accused killer in person, Reg believed that Spencer was the same man he'd once seen hanging around the heavily wooded trails at Four Mile Run Park, where he and Sue would go jogging. The man had stood out in his memory because he was alone and wasn't wearing athletic gear or walking; he had just been standing near one of the bends in the trail, acting suspiciously, Reg says.

It's worth nothing that retired Arlington homicide detective Joe Horgas thinks this is impossible; Spencer was released to the halfway house in Richmond in early September and the only documented time he went home to visit his relatives in Arlington was during the Thanksgiving weekend that Sue Tucker was murdered. Spencer had arrived in Arlington on Thanksgiving morning and had gotten a ride back to the halfway house in Richmond from his uncle three days later, on Sunday November 29, 1987. Reg, who had returned to Arlington from Wales for a couple weeks in September 1987, maintains he saw Spencer in the park.

It's never been determined how, when or where Spencer chose Sue Tucker as his next victim. (In testimony during the trial, Spencer's family stated that he had gone shopping at a nearby mall because he said he wanted to buy Christmas presents for family members, so that's certainly another possibility.)

"It's not impossible that he could have been stalking [her] at Four Mile Run," Reg says, "Could it have been somebody else? That's true. But I actually do think it was him."

A slew of DNA and forensic science experts also testified at the trial, discussing both the collection of the evidence and explaining the DNA testing process in detail. One of those expert witnesses included a future Nobel laureate: Sir Richard John Roberts, a British biochemist and molecular biologist who worked with James Watson at his Cold Spring Harbor Laboratory facility in New York.

Michael Baird, Ph.D., senior scientist and laboratory director at Lifecodes, the private New York lab that had performed the DNA testing, told reporters at the courthouse that "really, DNA is on trial along with the defendant."

The Arlington jury hearing the evidence was, on the whole, educated and affluent. Its members included a computer analyst and a lawyer who had formerly worked as an engineer. They were more than up to the task set before them.

"We did not strike gold with our jury," notes Womack, who'd hoped for a less-informed pool of jurors. "I wore pink socks. I had shocking pink socks on the day that they presented all this [DNA] evidence, just to try and distract the jury from this. And every time I got a chance, I'd pull up my pants … [and] I'd cross my legs."

Aside from possibly being distracted by Womack's pink socks, the Richmond prosecutors and defense attorneys sitting in the gallery were studiously paying attention to how Helen Fahey and Art Karp argued the prosecution's case.

Another thing the Richmonders couldn't fail to notice was how lax the security in Arlington was. By comparison, at the height of the

Richmond South Side Strangler trials, snipers would be posted on one courthouse roof and armed corrections officers would be stationed in the courtroom, say Richmond-area attorneys Jeff Everhart and David Johnson. Everhart was the lead attorney representing Spencer in his trials for the murders of Debbie Davis, Dr. Susan Hellams and Diane Cho. Johnson was his co-counsel on the Davis and Hellams murder trials.

"It was his best chance to escape, right?" Everhart asks. "They did a lot of sidebars. There was probably a 60-year-old deputy sheriff standing between [Spencer] and the door."

"Courtroom security was a lot different back then," Johnson agrees.

Perhaps the strongest evidence the prosecution had apart from the DNA was the fact that Timothy Spencer had been furloughed from the halfway house in Richmond to visit his family in Arlington during the Thanksgiving weekend murder of Sue Tucker.

Womack says that argument was far from the weakest circumstantial case he'd ever seen – especially given the fact that he himself wasn't able to account for Spencer's whereabouts during the murder.

Spencer was quiet around Womack and didn't volunteer loads of information for his own defense. He maintained his innocence and claimed that he had been with his family the entire Thanksgiving weekend but that didn't check out.

"We couldn't provide him with a complete alibi," Womack says. "They went to see his brother's basketball game, leaving him at home for about two hours … in the relevant time period." Spencer had no alibi for that timeframe, as well as for the late-night hours when his family had been sleeping.

During the sentencing portion of the trial, when Spencer's mother, Thelma, was questioned by defense attorneys about her son, she was asked, "Can you think of anything you might have done or would have done that might have made it all turn out different?"

"Yes," she replied. "I shouldn't have called him and invited him here for Thanksgiving in November."

After deliberating for five hours, the jury returned guilty verdicts against Timothy Spencer in the rape and murder of Sue Tucker.

It was a career-building case for Fahey, who would go on to be appointed by President Bill Clinton as U.S. Attorney for the Eastern District of Virginia, a coveted, high-profile position she would hold for almost eight years. During her time as one of the nation's top federal prosecutors, she would oversee the prosecutions of some of the biggest espionage cases in U.S. history, as CIA officers Aldrich Ames and Jim Nicholson were convicted for spying on the United States for the Soviet and Russian intelligence agencies. She also assisted in the investigation and arrest of FBI agent Robert Hanssen, another Soviet and Russian spy. One of Fahey's star employees in the Eastern District was future FBI Director James Comey, who, as an assistant U.S. attorney, managed her Richmond office.

The day after the verdict was handed down, on Saturday July 16, 1988, the Spencer jury returned and spent all day hearing testimony as to whether Spencer merited the death penalty for killing Sue Tucker.

Mulling it over for a little more than an hour, the jury sentenced him to death, prompting the one display of anger Timothy Spencer showed during the entire trial.

"He flipped the court off. He walked out and flipped the court off," Womack says.

It was unquestionably the first capital murder conviction in the United States based on DNA evidence and that alone would make it an historic, landmark verdict.

It also marked the first time in the world that a serial killer had been caught and convicted with DNA.

And though there has been some confusion on this point, the Spencer trial also holds the distinction of being the first time in United States history that DNA had been used to secure a conviction in *any murder case*.

Prior to the Spencer conviction, one killer in the entire world had been identified by DNA testing in England in 1987 but because he confessed and pleaded guilty, there had been no trial.

In February 1988, United States serial rapist Tommie Lee Andrews, who was suspected of two-dozen masked home-invasion rapes in Florida, became the first U.S. criminal convicted with DNA evidence.

Leading forensics expert acknowledge that the Spencer case was the first DNA murder case in U.S. history but there have also been media reports mistakenly lending that distinction to an Albany, New York case.

In 2017 there were some incorrect news reports online that a September 1987 New York murder had been the first DNA case. But in fact, the defendant in that case, George Wesley, wasn't found guilty until January 1989, six months after Timothy Spencer had already been convicted. (Lifecodes – the same private New York laboratory that tested the DNA evidence in the Timothy Spencer murders – also conducted the testing for the Andrews and Wesley cases.)

The confusion, however, demonstrates that even though the verdict against Timothy Spencer was a watershed for modern criminal justice, it is a case that has languished in obscurity for the past 30 years, despite the fact that it was reported on by *The New York Times*, *The Washington Post* and other major news outlets of the day.

And it also set lasting legal precedents "for DNA to be used in the courtroom, so that today you don't have to put on all your expert witnesses and prove DNA. It's accepted now," says retired Arlington homicide detective Joe Horgas.

Even though he'd already received one death sentence, Timothy Spencer refused to plead guilty to the other three murder charges he still faced.

Prosecutors were not going to offer Spencer any plea bargains. The families of his victims demanded justice. And because DNA evidence was still so new and police and prosecutors believed Spencer was a danger to society, prosecutors wanted to secure multiple capital convictions against him in the unlikely case any of Spencer's future appeals against the DNA science might prove successful.

Going to trial, though, meant that the victims' families would have to relive the trauma again and again. Susan Hellams' widower, Marcel Slag, would have to testify about coming home to discover his strangled wife's still-warm body. And Debbie Davis' father, Bill Dudley, spent what would have been Debbie's 36th birthday testifying in court about being the last person to speak to his daughter before her murder.

"It was very difficult," recalls Bill Dudley's nephew-in-law, Eric Fiske. "Bill and Josie left the courtroom when the medical examiner got on the stand and explained the medical aspects of [Debbie's] death. Bill and Josie couldn't stand that. It was a very tough week for them."

When Spencer's first death penalty verdict was handed down, Bill Dudley was quoted by the *Richmond Times-Dispatch* as saying that he hoped that Spencer would also get the death penalty for Debbie's murder. Dudley had recently been diagnosed with prostate cancer and had retired from his job as a heating and air conditioning repairman.

"You can't kill a man but one time," Dudley said, "but [the death sentence] will prove [Spencer] is a vicious killer."

Richmond Commonwealth's Attorney Aubrey Davis, who passed away in 2016, and former Richmond Assistant Commonwealth's Attorney Jack Driscoll prosecuted Spencer for the murders of Debbie Davis and Susan Hellams. The average inner-city Richmond juror back then didn't have much formal education and so Driscoll knew he couldn't use the same science-heavy approach in Richmond that was favored by the prosecution in Arlington.

Instead, Driscoll's strategy was to simplify the argument: When Timothy Spencer committed the murders he left behind a "calling card" – his own DNA, Driscoll told the jury. And there are people who can read that DNA, just like a fingerprint.

From there, Driscoll would dazzle the jurors with an array of impressive, top-notch scientists, professors and medical experts.

All you had to know, Driscoll says, is that the guys who were on the stand were super-smart, super-knowledgeable experts in their fields and that they relied on DNA in their jobs. "You get that across," says the retired prosecutor and judge, "and then you've won your case."

As for the defense, Jeff Everhart and David Johnson's approach was also simple: "Try to cast doubt on a new science," Everhart says.

"Because, in our case, that's all there was," says Johnson. "We were pointing out as best we can there's nothing else here – this is all they have. It's really brand-new and untested."

One of the lead witnesses for the prosecution was Michael Baird, the laboratory director from Lifecodes. Baird, who holds a doctorate in genetics, testified that there was only a one in 135 million chance that the DNA found at the crime scene would match any African-American male other than Timothy Spencer. At that time, the entire African-American population in the United States was only about 29 million.

"They used some awfully big numbers," Johnson says.

In 1988, there were no government criminal DNA databases in existence. So labs like Lifecodes were basing their odds calculations on the relatively small amount of DNA samples they had on file, sometimes only a thousand or more samples. Everhart and Dave Johnson were concerned that the scientists were vastly overinflating their estimates. But due to the fact that some of the leading DNA experts in the nation were testifying for the prosecution, the defense attorneys couldn't find any witnesses to contradict them.

"It would have been nice to have had an expert to help us, but we could not get anybody to help," Everhart says.

"It wasn't just that it was new," Johnson says. "The prosecution pulled out all the stops, and their experts were superstars in the science community at the time."

By January 20, 1989, Spencer had been found guilty for the rapes and murders of *Style Weekly* magazine accounts manager Debbie Davis, Medical College of Virginia neurosurgery resident Dr. Susan Hellams and U.S. Department of Agriculture magazine editor Sue Tucker.

He now had three death sentences levied against him.

After Spencer was convicted for Debbie Davis' murder, Spencer's younger brother Travis, then 17, took the witness stand during the sentencing hearing and testified that "DNA took my brother."

Richmond Commonwealth's Attorney Aubrey Davis shot back a correction, telling the jury, "DNA did not take his brother's life. DNA found the killer of three women. Timothy Spencer has put his life in jeopardy. ... Timothy Spencer deserves no mercy."

Twenty years later, when he was interviewed by British true-crime TV series *Born to Kill?*, Travis Spencer's stance on his older brother had evolved. "I think something wasn't really right in [his] mind," Travis said. "If somebody's ill ... [they need] treatment ... with medication, some doctoring. ... Growing up in that household, he was definitely ill."

Less than four months later, in May 1989, Spencer would stand trial for the murder of 15-year-old Manchester High School freshman Diane Cho.

This last trial is especially notable for the fact that it marked the first time in the world that polymerase chain reaction (PCR) DNA testing was introduced as evidence in a murder trial.

Contaminated with menstrual blood and bacteria, the semen samples recovered from the Cho murder scene weren't as large or pure as the samples recovered from some of the other murders.

So, lacking a good DNA sample, the prosecution's strategy this time around was to prove that the method of Diane Cho's murder matched more than 12 signatures associated with Spencer's ritualistic M.O. as a convicted serial killer. These included breaking in through a window, specific methods of binding his victims and covering the victims' buttocks and private areas after they'd been raped and murdered.

Discussing the fact that Spencer had covered the genitals and buttocks of Diane Cho, Susan Tucker and Debbie Davis after their murders, Chesterfield County Deputy Commonwealth's Attorney Warren Von Schuch told the jurors, "I cannot tell the court whether it was denial or shame, or whether it's street-wise, trying to make the [crime] scene look as normal as possible. I don't know. But in each one of these cases there was a deliberate effort to conceal … part of the body that was totally unnecessary; it was totally willful and it was subsequent to the commission of the crime. That, I submit, is a signature in … these crimes that tell you something in the [killer's] subconscious [mind]."

In addition to arguing that all of the murders were uniquely alike, the prosecution also introduced the new cutting-edge PCR DNA testing process, which could amplify degraded DNA samples. In 1989, PCR testing was still new and nowhere near as refined as it is today, so while the amplified sample from the Cho murder did match Spencer's DNA, at that time scientists could only give one in 100 odds for the sample belonging to anyone but Spencer.

Nevertheless, this breakthrough testing method would go on to win the Nobel Prize for Chemistry in 1993. And the next time it made big news would be in 1994, when it was used in the O.J. Simpson trial. Today, PCR is the most commonly used DNA testing method, allowing scientists to replicate DNA and make more of it available for testing.

Aside from being another landmark moment for forensic science, the Cho murder trial also yielded some dramatic moments straight out of a courtroom movie: It began when Diane Cho's mother, Hyun Kyoung Cho, took the witness stand to recount how she'd found her daughter's body. Mrs. Cho became rattled by seeing Spencer in person. Speaking through a court-certified Korean translator, she asked the judge if she could say a prayer before her testimony.

"What are you going to say? It's hard to object to that," Everhart says.

"I just asked for time to pray and I was praying," Mrs. Cho says. While she can't recollect everything she said in her prayer, "I remember one thing: Please let him repent and let him speak honestly [about] what he did to my daughter."

As Everhart recalls, Diane Cho's mother "started speaking in Korean. And I don't understand Korean. But as she prayed, her voice started to rise and very loudly. And she screams, 'Spenc—er!!'"

Hyun Kyoung Cho broke down during the trial for her daughter's murder when bailiffs tried to retrieve Diane's photo from her to place it back into evidence.

Former Chesterfield County prosecutor Billy Davenport, who argued the Cho murder case with Von Schuch, says the prayer "was so emotional that some of the jurors and some of us had tears in our eyes because of the heartfelt impact of her grief that came through no matter the language."

During questioning, Davenport handed Mrs. Cho a photo of Diane, and she clutched the image of her daughter to her breast, sobbing. Deputies had to retrieve the picture from her when she wouldn't return it to be submitted into evidence, which made her cry harder.

Davenport called for a break.

And then, as Mrs. Cho stepped down from the witness stand and walked past the defense table, something snapped inside of her.

She lunged at Spencer, screaming.

"It was like my heart was bursting," she remembers. "My chest is just exploding."

Davenport ran between Diane's mother and Spencer, separating them, while the court bailiff and armed officers secured Spencer. Because Spencer was a high-profile death row inmate and considered dangerous, the court was guarded by sheriff's deputies and plainclothes police as well as state correctional guards.

"I actually wanted to kill him," Mrs. Cho says. "My daughter was just full of future. Why did you do that? Why did you do that to my daughter? She is just full of hope and future. She has so much to offer. And I couldn't control myself."

Due to the outburst, Davenport excused Mrs. Cho from any further testimony. The defense expressed concern that her tears and anger would sway the jury.

"That was the only time I went to court," says Mrs. Cho.

Later that same day, as a thunderstorm was passing over the area, a Richmond detective was showing the jury crime-scene photos from the Davis and Hellams murders when the lights suddenly went out, plunging the courtroom into complete darkness.

What followed next was utter chaos, says defense attorney Jeff Everhart: "You heard holsters unsnap, the judge took a dive. Spencer was to my right and I said, 'Don't move. Whatever you do, *do not move*. And I'm telling you, the people in the courtroom screamed. It was Bizarro World. That was one of the most ... eeriest experiences in my entire life."

In the court's adjoining witness room, Ray Williams opened the door into the courtroom to find out what was going on. "The judge said, 'Don't anybody move! Take charge of the prisoner!'" Ray says.

The jurors wanted out of there, Davenport remembers. The tension was unbelievable. It seemed like an eternity before the emergency lights kicked in, but it was really only a few seconds.

And that wasn't the only unnerving moment during the eight-day trial. In fact, at one point, the entire courtroom was evacuated due to a terrorist bomb threat that had been called in to multiple area courthouses.

The lead attorney for all three of Spencer's Richmond-area capital murder trials, Jeff Everhart struggled with doubts about whether Spencer had committed the murders.

Finally, on Friday, May 12, 1989, after deliberating for nearly four hours, the jury made its decision, finding Spencer guilty for the rape and murder of Diane Cho.

Jeff Everhart would argue against the death penalty, telling jurors it wasn't necessary because, with three death sentences under his belt, his client was already "a walking dead man."

But after just 47 minutes of consideration, the jury handed down Spencer's fourth and final death sentence.

Timothy Spencer, the South Side Strangler, had been on trial for almost 10 months straight.

"The other thing I remember is Timothy Spencer's mother in Chesterfield saying, 'It's like going to a play. You see the same play over and over and you know the outcome,'" Everhart recalls.

"Those cases were all exhausting. And even though you kind of expect or anticipate the results, I mean, let's not kid ourselves: A jury would be hard-pressed to give a person life having heard the circumstances and the details and seeing the pictures of those women's demise. Those women all suffered. I mean, these were not quick deaths."

❖

In the year that he spent on trial for the four murders, Timothy Spencer's emotionless public façade only slipped a few times, notably at his February 27, 1989, death penalty sentencing hearing for the murder of Hellams, when he took the witness stand and angrily railed against the DNA scientists and claimed he'd been framed by prosecutors and Arlington Detective Joe Horgas.

"You think it's funny? You getting it back," he said, glowering at city prosecutors Davis and Driscoll. "My name ain't Timothy Spencer [if I don't] prove you set me up."

Dressed in his denim prison uniform with his handcuffed wrists chained to his waist, Spencer fumed, telling Judge James Wilkinson, "You watch, your honor, all this little DNA stuff y'all brought up in here, I'm gonna show you how these low-life people came up here [and] call me a murderer. I'm going to show you these people came in here, tried to play God, but God doesn't call for me yet. ... I'm gonna prove these people set me up."

When Wilkinson asked who set him up, Spencer retorted, "You will find out, your honor. I ain't being smart to you, but they know what is going on, and everybody else will know in time."

Spencer had previously lashed out at Horgas during his November 1988 sentencing hearing for the murder of Sue Tucker. Taking the witness stand then, Spencer said, "I would just like to say I am sorry that my family is going through this. I feel sorry for the person who got killed and her family. I would like to get a chance to prove I ain't this sort of person. Detective Horgas set me up because this [DNA] is nothing but a fake. This is all I've got to say."

Asked by the judge if there was any reason the court should not affirm the death sentence, Spencer said, "Yes, because Detective Horgas set me up for this thing. ... [The DNA] didn't match anything. He ran tests from the Richmond police. [The Arlington police] ain't even do it theirselves. I've gone through two trial[s] already. I done seen how he did it. I'm asking you to give me the chance to prove it – that I didn't do what I'm being sentenced for today."

Asked once more if there was any reason why the judge should not impose the sentence, Spencer simply replied, "Because I'm innocent."

❖

Given the fact that Spencer maintained his innocence throughout four capital murder trials, one may reasonably wonder: Is there any chance he didn't do it?

Jeff Everhart and Dave Johnson say at the time they defended Spencer, they weren't sure.

"I always have had some doubts – doubts along the lines of what could we have done differently, what could we have done better? And was he really guilty?" Everhart says. "The scientific evidence tells you he's guilty, but at least for me, I always had some residual doubt."

"I think a lot of that came from Timothy," Johnson says. "I mean, he was a very good client: polite, quiet, not demanding, insistent on his innocence."

Everhart and Johnson decided on an extraordinary course of action: Before the first Richmond case went to trial, they surreptitiously submitted a sample of Spencer's blood to a North Carolina DNA testing lab under a false name and asked the lab to compare Spencer's DNA to the DNA profile of the killer.

"We arranged to have a sample of his blood sent to a lab in Winston-Salem, North Carolina, that did paternity testing," explains Everhart. "And it came back that it was him."

Arlington defense attorney Carl Womack concedes that the science proved Spencer was unequivocally guilty.

He's proud of giving Spencer a vigorous defense because everyone is entitled to that under the U.S. Constitution. But losing the case, Womack believes, also served justice.

"Tim Spencer was ..." Womack begins hesitantly before amending his words and continuing: "*Whoever* did those [crimes] was not a good person [and] in many respects, certainly didn't deserve to walk on the face of the earth with free people anymore."

CHAPTER 8

THE WRONG MAN

Carolyn Hamm's secretary was worried. It was Wednesday, January 25, 1984, and for the second day in a row, Carolyn hadn't show up for work. She had also missed several appointments, which was not at all characteristic of the hard-working young attorney. Finally, her secretary decided to call Carolyn's best friend, Darla Henry.

Darla had just seen Carolyn two nights before, on Monday evening at the Capitol Hill Squash Club. Considering the fact that Carolyn was preparing to fly to Peru that weekend for a long vacation, Darla thought she might have just been preoccupied with errands. But she promised Carolyn's secretary that she'd go over and check on Carolyn during lunch.

When Darla arrived at Carolyn's Arlington, Virginia, home, her young lawyer friend's blue Plymouth Horizon hatchback was still parked in the driveway of her white clapboard home. Walking to the porch, Darla could see the front door was slightly open. Snow had spread into the front entryway, partially covering the envelopes that had accumulated on the floor below the mail slot.

Now Darla's pulse was quickening.

Scared and spotting a young neighbor across the street getting ready to leave in his car, Darla called him over and asked if he would help her investigate. As the two tentatively entered the house, Darla

132

was aghast to find Carolyn's empty purse at the bottom of the stairs, its ransacked contents dumped on the floorboards.

There was no sign of Carolyn; her workout clothes from two nights before were still on the bathroom floor upstairs. Downstairs, discarded on the living room rug, they found Carolyn's dark-blue terrycloth robe. In the kitchen, they discovered lengths of cut stereo wire and Venetian blind cords draped over a chair.

Descending with Carolyn's young neighbor into the basement, Darla immediately noticed a freezing draft. Someone had ripped the dryer duct out of the laundry room window, leaving it wide open to the brisk winter air.

In the hallway leading to the garage, that same someone had partly unfurled a rolled-up rug and left a kitchen steak knife resting on top of it.

And then, Darla spotted the body.

Carolyn's ghostly white bare feet were lying just inside the doorway leading from the basement to the garage. Her naked body was face-down on the garage floor, her wrists bound tightly behind her back with Venetian blind cords. She had been strangled with a noose fashioned from a heavy hemp rope that had been cut from around the rolled-up carpet in the hallway. The Strangler had tossed the other end of the rope over a water pipe and tied it securely to the bumper of Carolyn's broken-down blue Fiat, which she kept in the garage. The ropes had been secured with reef and half-hitch knots – basic knots common to scouting programs.

The murder scene itself was strangely neat and bloodless. With her head resting on the concrete garage floor and her eyes shut, Carolyn Hamm almost looked like she could have been sleeping.

"It shattered … it really just destroyed our family. It was devastating," says Carolyn Hamm's older sister, Joan McCloskey.

Their father, Wilbur Hamm, an accountant and engineer, and their mother, Jean, who had been the dean of students at the Muhlenberg Nursing School in Plainfield, New Jersey, were informed of the murder by a state policeman who was dispatched to their home.

"My mother didn't want to hear it," McCloskey remembers. "She was pounding the cop and beating him on his chest. ... And my grandmother, who was over 96 at the time, it was impossible to comfort her, because she's going, 'Why me? Why me? Why didn't God take me?' And it affected every member of my family: cousins, aunts, uncles. Everyone was affected by it.

"It was hard to believe. And the more you learned about it, the worse it got."

Carolyn Hamm's greatest fear had been that someone would break into her house and kill her.

While that's not an uncommon anxiety among women, Carolyn had shared that unsettling secret with one of her friends just two weeks before her bound and strangled body was discovered in her garage.

An ambitious young attorney, Carolyn Hamm worked at Wilkes, Artis, Hedrick & Lane, the oldest real estate law firm in the Washington, D.C., metropolitan area. (*Photo courtesy Joan McCloskey*)

A promising young lawyer at the Washington, D.C., law firm of Wilkes, Artis, Hedrick & Lane, Carolyn wasn't afraid of breaking glass ceilings. She was among the first class of women admitted into

Princeton in 1969. And she organized and captained Princeton's first women's crew team.

"At Princeton she was one of 10 women who transferred in [during] the first year they accepted women and she went out for crew and that was the first time they had any women on the Princeton crew team," says her sister. "I think people gave her a hard time on that. The coach was not thrilled at having women and I think he made them work harder than he should have."

McCloskey remembers her younger sister as a vivacious, intelligent and ardent world traveler. Carolyn had vacationed with their mother to Egypt, where the two women rode camels to the pyramids. At the time of her murder, Carolyn was preparing to travel to Peru to tour the Incan ruins at Machu Picchu.

In her professional life, Carolyn Hamm was a passionate historic preservationist. After graduating from Princeton in 1973, she went on to earn her master's degree from Cornell, focusing on architectural history, urban development and preservation planning. While pursuing her law degree at Duke, she took a year off from her studies to work for the National Trust for Historic Preservation and the National Register of Historic Places.

Carolyn Hamm

"She always had a beautiful smile. She was very attractive physically and personality-wise. She was a perfectionist. She had excellent grades all through school. She graduated magna cum laude," McCloskey says proudly. "But she worked hard for it. It didn't come easy to her."As an attorney, Carolyn had already carved out a valuable niche practice in historic preservation law. In 1982 she took a year's sabbatical from her law firm to serve as acting head of the University of Vermont's historic preservation graduate program.

"She was very much interested in learning [and was] fascinated with architecture and history. She took hundreds of pictures of things like old door knobs and hinges and lamps and gaslights and things that I would just walk by. But she would categorize them and learn from them. She was very much into art history," her sister recalls.

Active and athletic, Carolyn Hamm dabbled in photography and pottery-making and enjoyed jogging, horseback riding, skiing and playing squash. She was a Beach Boys fan who also appreciated Vivaldi.

Just 32 at the time of her death in January 1984, she might have gone on to become a law professor or to head up an historic preservation nonprofit. Instead, she would become the first woman to meet a cruel and brutal end at the hands of Timothy Spencer, the future South Side Strangler.

Lacking fingerprints or any obvious suspects, Arlington County homicide detectives at first focused their attention on the young neighbor who'd found Carolyn Hamm's body with Darla Henry, says retired Arlington County homicide detective Joe Horgas.

"Well, after about a week or so of not solving the case, Arlington police brought this kid in and they interrogated him," Horgas says. "And what do you think he told his family when he got home? 'They think *I* did it! The police think *I* did it!'"

At the point the police asked for hair and blood samples, Horgas says, "Lo and behold, what happens bright and early the next day? This guy's sister calls Arlington police to report, 'Hey, I just want you to know that I was a friend of Carolyn Hamm and I remember talking to her. She told me she was out sunbathing in the backyard and she sees this guy [David] Vasquez who lived in the neighborhood out like a peeping Tom, looking at her.'"

In fact, the young man's sister told police, she had seen Vasquez walking in front of Hamm's house that Monday night, just two days before Carolyn Hamm's body was found. Vasquez, she told police, was "creepy."

Essentially, Horgas says, the sister was telling the police, "Don't look at my brother. Look at this other guy, Vasquez."

David Vasquez had indeed lived in the same neighborhood as Carolyn Hamm, bordering Arlington's 65-acre Barcroft Park. But he had moved away in May 1983, more than seven months before Hamm was murdered.

David was 37 at the time of the killing, but with an IQ below 70, he functioned intellectually at about the level of a 10-year-old child, depending on the situation.

At the time of the murder, David was living 25 miles away in Manassas, Virginia, where he worked as a janitor at a local McDonald's fast-food restaurant and lived with his mother, Imelda Shapiro, a local telephone company employee who went by the nickname Mel.

Later, another witness, a retired Army colonel, would come forward claiming that he too had seen David Vasquez in the neighborhood, this time on the Wednesday that Hamm's body was found.

However, putting aside the fact that the Hamm murder has now been officially attributed to Timothy Spencer, there are other problems with witnesses saying they saw David Vasquez near Hamm's house that January.

David lived 25 miles away and due to his mental disability, he couldn't drive. His mother swore to police and friends that he hadn't been outside of Manassas that week. And David didn't really have any friends who would have driven him from Manassas to Arlington, says family friend Julie Bennett Cooke.

"David was just one of the sweetest people you'd ever want to meet and he was very childlike," Cooke says. "David used to live in Arlington but then he was living with his mom at the time. Now how in the world could he have gotten from Manassas to Arlington on a bitter cold night? And he didn't drive. None of us could ever figure that out."

Searching the bedroom where David had lived with neighbors before moving to his mother's home in Manassas, homicide detectives found some nudie magazines and racy photos. One of these magazines featured an interior photo of a tied-up, gagged woman with rope encircling her neck. There was also an envelope of snapshots, evidently surreptitiously taken by David, of local women in swimsuits and cutoff shorts. These included photos of teen lacrosse and girls' soccer players from the local high school. Nevertheless, the only blemish on David's criminal record up until that point was a minor theft charge: When he was 19, David had been caught stealing some coins from a laundromat.

Arlington homicide detective Bob Carrig was the lead investigator on the case. Before he became aware of David Vasquez, Carrig had at first briefly entertained the notion that Hamm might have been the victim of an accidental suicide by autoerotic asphyxiation. But the medical examiner ruled out that possibility – in addition to having her hands tightly bound behind her, she had clearly been murdered and raped. The killer had left Vaseline around her mouth and vagina and semen was discovered on her body as well on the discarded bathrobe in her living room.

David Vasquez initially denied being in the area or having anything to do with the murders, but over several hours of interrogations on three separate days, Carrig got David to confess to murdering Carolyn Hamm.

However, Horgas and many others say there were serious problems with David's confessions.

"They spent hours and hours with him and there's transcripts of all this," Horgas says. "So I think it was Carrig that basically got to a point [of] you know, 'You killed her.' 'OK, I killed her.' 'How did you kill her?' 'I stabbed her.' 'No, no, no, no, you put a rope around…' 'Oh yeah, yeah, yeah, yeah, that's right.' 'How did you get in?' 'I broke the window.' 'No, no, no, no, you did *this*.'

"He doesn't know anything, but he's being *told* how he supposedly did it. He then regurgitates everything Carrig told them on how he did it. He is now saying, 'This is how I did it.' And that was the confession."

Joe Horgas' recollection of the interrogation is not exact or verbatim, of course, but reading excerpts of the Vasquez interrogation transcripts, it seems reasonably close to how the questioning actually went down.

For starters, Carrig and another detective, Chuck Shelton, began the interview by lying to David Vasquez. They told David that they had found his fingerprints at the crime scene, which left David understandably confused. In actuality, there was no evidence connecting David Vasquez to the murder, aside from the testimony of the two neighbors who claimed to have seen him walking around the area.

When the detectives asked David how he had gotten there, David said he wanted to know too: "Because my mom was working and she can't drive, and I don't drive."

At one point in the interrogation, Shelton said to David, "Tell us how you did it."

"I grabbed the knife and just stabbed her, that's all," David replied.

"Oh, David, no, David!" Carrig exclaimed. "Now if you would have told us the way it happened, we could believe you a little bit better."

"I only say that it did happen and I did it, my fingerprints were on it," David answered.

"You hung her," Carrig said.

"What?" David asked.

"You hung her!" insisted Carrig.

"Okay, so I hung her," David parroted back to the homicide detective.

Later, the detectives asked David what he used to bind Carolyn Hamm's hands. David helpfully offered that he used his belt, and they told him, no, try again. Then David said it was a rope, and then he changed his answer to a coat hanger. Finally, after several exchanges, a seemingly exasperated Carrig said, "No, it wasn't a coat hanger. It was something *like* a coat hanger. What was it? By the window? Think about the Venetian blinds, David. Remember cutting the Venetian blind cord?"

During David Vasquez's first interrogation, the two detectives had not yet advised David of his Miranda rights. On the second day, Vasquez revealed to the detectives that he had "horrible dreams" about murdering Hamm, describing the murder scenario he had been fed in the previous interrogation. David would later describe his nightmare to police a second time after signing a Miranda waiver.

"Girl was in my dream, it's a horrible dream, too horrible," David told Carrig and Shelton.

"I got myself in hell by breaking glass. The dryer was hooked up, cut my hand in glass. I need help, then I went upstairs, she kept coming out. She startled me. I startled her. We both kinda screamed a little bit. She told me, what was I doing? I said, 'I came over to see you.' She wanted to make love. She said 'yes' and 'no' and then said, 'okay' and we went upstairs to her bedroom, kissed a little and then took each other's clothes off. ... She told me, would I tie her hands? She said, 'There's a knife in the kitchen, cut string off the blinds, just tie me.' Then I asked her ... if it's too tight. She said no ... [I] walk downstairs ... took her pictures, she's nice. She said, 'Tie me some more.' ... I brought ... some big rope and ... she told me 'The other way.' I says, 'What way is that?' She says, 'By hanging.' I says, 'No, don't have to hang, no, no, no, no.' She said 'yes' and called me a chicken. So I did it. ... I don't want my dream anymore. That dream, too much."

At the time he was arrested for Carolyn Hamm's murder in 1984, David Vasquez had been working as a janitor at a McDonald's about 25 miles away in Manassas, Virginia.

On February 6, 1984, David Vasquez was charged with the rape and murder of Carolyn Hamm, as well as burglarizing her home.

Later, in pre-trial hearings, a judge threw out Vasquez's first two confessions, which had been obtained before he signed a waiver of his Miranda rights. The second of David's two so-called "dream confessions" was allowed into evidence.

"There's absolutely no way possible any of us thought that David could have done it," says Cooke, the family friend. "David was a tiny little guy. There's no way he could have done what they said. And they really tricked him into confessing and that was horrible."

Due to David's reduced mental faculties, police didn't think he had committed the crime on his own, explains Helen Fahey, who was elected as Arlington County Commonwealth's Attorney a couple years after David Vasquez was arrested.

"First of all, David Vasquez was a small, slight individual," Fahey says. "The confession was not a good confession in part because of who David Vasquez was, the type of person he was. There were a lot of issues in the confession and he confessed essentially three different times to the police. And there were inconsistencies and a lot of issues.

"He was borderline retarded and did not appear to be emotionally a very strong person. And the murder of Carolyn Hamm was obviously a planned, complicated murder and when they ran the blood [tests on the semen sample] from the crime scene, it did not match David Vasquez. So the theory was that there must have been two people involved in the Carolyn Hamm murder."

But police could never get Vasquez to tell them who that second theoretical person had been.

They interviewed and took blood samples from four men who had been friends with Vasquez, including a man who had been institutionalized and had a history of peeping Tom incidents. None of their blood types matched the semen sample from the Hamm murder scene either. (Before DNA came along, the cutting-edge method of matching a rapist or murderer to a crime scene was through serology and blood typing. About 80 percent of people secrete their ABO blood types into bodily fluids such as semen and saliva. Spencer was a Type O secretor and his blood contained enzymes that were a match for about 13 percent of the

U.S. population, or about 3.1 million Americans in 1987. That was far less accurate than the DNA testing performed on Spencer, which determined that his DNA was a 1-in-135 million match for the South Side Strangler's DNA, more than enough to definitively declare him the killer.)

Vasquez's own defense attorney was reportedly convinced of his client's guilt after a physician injected Vasquez with sodium amytal – the so-called truth serum – and Vasquez *still* confessed to the murder. These days, however, the notion of truth serum has been discredited and experts now believe that sodium amytal can actually influence the creation of *false* memories.

But on the basis of this sodium amytal-assisted confession and David's "dream confession" to police, his defense attorney recommended that David enter an Alford plea. That's a plea in which the defendant doesn't admit their guilt but concedes that there is enough evidence to convict them for the crime.

David Vasquez was sentenced to 35 years in prison for the murder of Carolyn Hamm.

And even though he had sincerely believed that David Vasquez was involved in the murder, Detective Bob Carrig didn't feel good about the outcome.

"The kid shouldn't have been in jail. He didn't have enough brains to come in out of the rain. But there was what it was. You know, I didn't stand up there and take the Alford plea. That's the sad part of the whole case," says the now-retired Carrig. "That was a sad day for criminal justice. I felt bad for Vasquez in that moment. I felt bad when he was convicted or when he took the Alford plea. I felt bad for him."

David was incarcerated at Buckingham Correctional Facility in Dillwyn, Virginia, about two-and-a-half hours away from his mother, Mel. She had a daughter who'd died in childhood and with David in prison, she was now all alone.

"It makes you want to cry," Mel told the Washington Post. "They didn't put a man in prison; they put a *child*."

The stress of knowing David had been wrongly imprisoned was too much on Mel, Julie Cooke says.

"The whole time that he was incarcerated, it just about killed his mother," Cooke remembers. "There was many times at the phone company when she would just stand up and pass out. We had to call the rescue squad so many times for her."

David wrote his mother and Julie while he was in the Buckingham prison. "I wish I kept his letters. He sent me the sweetest letters thanking me for taking care of his mom. That's all he cared about. It was really a horrible time," says Cooke.

Four years later, in November 1987, at the scene of the bondage rape and murder of Sue Tucker, Bob Carrig would remark to Joe Horgas that they'd seen this same type of murder before. It was Carolyn Hamm all over again.

When Horgas began reinvestigating the Hamm case, he interviewed David Vasquez in prison, where he learned that David had been raped behind bars. Horgas quickly determined that David had nothing to do with the Hamm murder.

And while Horgas was a great detective, he wasn't the most popular guy in his department. And telling his fellow detectives that they put an innocent man in prison wasn't exactly something his co-workers wanted to hear at first, he says: "Well, it was a touchy subject because, keep in mind, I'm working with the guys that put him away."

Horgas assembled a rock-solid case, proving that Timothy Spencer had been Arlington's Masked Rapist, as well as the serial killer known as the South Side Strangler. And while it is now accepted fact that Spencer murdered Carolyn Hamm, the semen sample on Hamm's bathrobe was too degraded to test for DNA with the technology available in 1988.

Furthermore, the witnesses who claimed to have seen David Vasquez in the neighborhood didn't change their stories, Bob Carrig says.

"We went back and reviewed the whole case over again with Carolyn Hamm. We re-interviewed all the witnesses, the witness that saw him standing outside the murder scene," Carrig says. "We had a colonel or a general or somebody from [the] CIA or something that saw him and I mean, anybody we talked to, they were reputable people. And you go back a year or whatever later, and they still have the same story. Nothing ever changed."

Carrig continues, asking, "Do I believe Spencer did it? Probably so, you know, but I can't prove it. They couldn't prove it or else he would have been charged with that one, I'm sure. There is nothing that takes Vasquez out of the crime and nothing that puts Spencer in the crime, you know? ... I don't know if Vasquez to this day did it or not. In my own heart, I don't believe he did. I believe Spencer did it, knowing everything that we know after all this investigation. However, there is no proof one way or the other for either one of them. And that's the bottom line."

As it became apparent to many law enforcement professionals that a miscarriage of justice had taken place against David Vasquez, Arlington prosecutor Helen Fahey was individually approached by Joe Horgas in Arlington, Ray Williams from the Richmond Police Department and Steve Mardigian from the FBI's Behavioral Science Unit. Each wanted to see what could be done to free David Vasquez.

"The gentleman had mental capacity challenges and, you know, the interview and interrogation was heavy and strong and he was overwhelmed, I think, and ... I don't think he had the best legal representation," says Mardigian.

Ray Williams recalls that "I went to Helen Fahey myself. I said, 'Y'all got the wrong guy.' He showed like a 70 IQ. I said, 'You can't leave that man in jail.' ... They knew he was retarded. You could tell him just anything you want to tell him [and] he was going to feed it back to you. In interviews with suspects, you have to watch what you tell them. I would never tell [a suspect] a fact in [a murder] case. He's got to tell me."

Summing up the case, Fahey says, "The physical evidence from the Carolyn Hamm crime scene was degraded to the point that they could not get DNA. So it was not possible to prove with DNA that it was Spencer or to exculpate David Vasquez. So that left us with David Vasquez in the penitentiary, where most people believed at that point that it had been Timothy Spencer, not Vasquez, but the evidence wasn't very convincing either way."

Mardigian and other agents from the FBI's Behavioral Science Unit put together a dossier that would prove that Carolyn Hamm's murder fit Spencer's M.O. as a serial killer as well as the geographic and chronological pattern of Spencer's other crimes.

That research would become the basis of an exhaustive, 12-page clemency request that Helen Fahey would submit to Virginia Governor Gerald Baliles in October 1988, petitioning the governor to free David Vasquez.

"When it was all said and done, we were able to link Timmy Spencer to four of the five homicides physically, forensically, with DNA. Unfortunately that opportunity didn't occur forensically with the Carolyn Hamm case and there was a man in jail," Mardigian says.

"But the similarities were demonstrative behaviorally [so] what we did in the [FBI] profiling unit was me and another gentleman that worked in the ViCAP [Violent Criminal Apprehension] program, spent a lot of time going through the particulars of all the crimes, all the homicides, all the burglaries, all the rapes [and] we did spreadsheets and picked out the salient points of each of the crimes. And I think ... John Douglas may have participated some too.

"We constructed an opinion that the individual that was responsible for the Carolyn Hamm case would not have had the, let's say, the lack of intellectual capacity that David Vasquez did and that the person that committed the other four crimes most likely was the person that committed the Hamm case. And we presented those findings to the governor at that time and I guess it was months going through this."

On January 4, 1989, citing "reason and justice," Virginia Governor Baliles granted David Vasquez a full pardon.

David had been imprisoned almost five years.

On the day David was released, the jury selection process was beginning in Timothy Spencer's trial for the murder of Dr. Susan Hellams.

The Virginia state legislature would later compensate David $117,000, which came out to a little more than $65 for each of the nearly 1,800 days he had been imprisoned.

Retired Arlington deputy prosecutor Art Karp remembers that one of the Arlington homicide detectives had asked if he could personally deliver the news of the pardon to David.

"As a matter of fact, one of the things that really touched me was … [Bob] Carrig came in," Karp remembers. "He came in to me and said, 'Art, please let me be the one to go down and tell this guy he's getting out.'"

"I was there when David came home," recalls Cooke. "I was at the house when David finally came home. We had a huge welcoming party for him. The news people were there. The homecoming was amazing. We were so excited, we were so happy. We had food. You know, it was a party. We were all thrilled. We didn't dwell on what had happened and where he was. We were just so thrilled that this happened. And then he was home and Mel was just so thankful to

In his later years, David Vasquez bagged groceries at a supermarket.

that detective [Horgas] as we all were, but she would say all the time if it wasn't for [Horgas] … Her love for him was just amazing. Mel appreciated him from the bottom of her heart. I think that he was an amazing man."

As for David, Cooke says, he "had no ill feelings. He carried no grudges. I remember him saying repeatedly, 'They just made a mistake.'"

Interviewed by *The Washington Post* shortly before he was released from prison, David said, "To me, it feels like a dream. It's just hard and all. It's been hard on my mother. She feels like she's been in here, too."

Asked about why he confessed, David told the *Post* that the police detectives "pushed me. They put words into my mouth. I was repeating everything they were saying."

Decades later, David still lived in fear that he would again be falsely accused of committing a crime and sent back to prison.

❖

Not everyone celebrated David's pardon and release, however.

For Carolyn Hamm's family, it was a painful and confusing time, reopening fresh wounds.

"My mother became even more upset. She couldn't understand," says Carolyn Hamm's older sister, Joan McCloskey. "I remember her saying, 'Why did they let that man go? Why did they let that man go?' And [me] telling her because he didn't do it. But she was really inconsolable."

Carolyn Hamm was among the first group of women admitted into Princeton. (*Photo courtesy Joan McCloskey*)

Almost 35 years after her sister's murder, Joan McCloskey is still grappling with her grief. "It's indescribable really, but for 25 years, I never told people who I was meeting for the first time that I had ever had a sister. I just didn't discuss it," she says.

Even when Spencer received the death penalty, there was never any sense of closure for Joan or for her parents: "They were never the same," McCloskey says. "My father was depressed and sort of turned inward. My mother struggled with it for a very long time. It took her a long, long time to come back to some kind of normalcy. But it was never, never the same."

As for David Vasquez's mother, she may have been grateful to Joe Horgas but she went to her grave harboring a grudge against the other Arlington police who put her son in prison. She passed away in 2006.

"We all were very angry but, yeah, she was incredibly angry. She hated those people until the day she died. She probably still does. I hope wherever she is, they don't cross her path," Cooke says.

David Vasquez died in 2013 at age 66.

In his later years, David worked as a grocery store bag boy. He had been taken in by neighbors who looked after him following his mother's death.

"Once his momma died, I don't think he really had much of a will to live," Cooke says, "because he and his mother were very close, especially after he got out of prison. You know, she was his life."

CHAPTER 9

THE DNA LEGACY

Sometimes one little mistake is all it takes to change your life forever.

For Debbie Smith, it was forgetting to lock the door behind her.

It was March 1989 and the stay-at-home mom was straightening up around her Williamsburg, Virginia, home, preparing to have friends over for dinner that evening when she noticed her clothes dryer wasn't working properly. So she went outside to check on the dryer exhaust vent.

Debbie's husband, Rob, a local police officer, was upstairs sleeping in the couple's bedroom. He had been on duty for 36 hours straight before he hit the bed and he was out for the count.

"As a police officer's wife, I knew you leave your doors locked, but I thought I'll just leave it unlocked for a few minutes when I came back in from checking the exhaust vent because I thought I will grab the trash and just come right back out," Debbie recalls. "But before I could come back out … a masked stranger came in that door [and] forcibly took me out of my home to the woods behind my house, where he robbed and repeatedly raped me.

"I really thought that he was going to shoot me," Debbie says, "because he said he had a gun. I never saw the gun because I was blindfolded and then, as I walked further, he said, 'And lady? … Lock your doors,' and those words sent chills up my spine and they do to this day."

When the ordeal had ended, the masked attacker marched the blindfolded Debbie Smith out of the woods and threatened to kill her and her family if she told anyone. "Remember: I know where you live and I will come back to kill you or your family if you tell anyone," the rapist said.

"But I did tell someone," Debbie says, crying from the memories. "As soon as I was allowed to leave those woods, I ran upstairs and I woke my husband with the only words I could get out of my mouth and all I could say was, 'He got me, Rob. He got me.'"

Rob Smith's first instinct was to report the rape and abduction to the police, Debbie Smith says. "And I begged him not to because I didn't want to get anybody else involved with this because I feared that this man really would come back and kill me or, worse, he may grab one of my children. My children were 12 and 13 at the time. But I'm thankful that my husband looked past my tears."

Rob told his wife, "Honey, you've got to go to the hospital. We need to talk to the police and then you need to go to the hospital and allow them to take the rape kit."

Debbie couldn't imagine going through the intrusive process after just having been raped, she says, but her husband "helped me to do what he knew that I couldn't do on my own that day and I will be forever grateful to him for helping me to do that," she says. "He refused to let my tears keep him from helping me to make those hard decisions."

Debbie's decision to allow evidence of the rape to be collected would turn out to be momentous – not only for herself and her family but also the nation.

The history of how DNA testing came to be law enforcement's top forensic investigative tool begins in 1980s England with a killer with the unlikely but unbelievably appropriate name of Colin

Pitchfork. The saga was chronicled in best-selling author Joseph Wambaugh's 1989 book *The Blooding*.

In November 1983, 15-year Lynda Mann was found raped and strangled to death on a lonely footpath called the Black Pad in the village of Narborough in Leicestershire, England. Two-and-a-half years later, the body of another raped and strangled 15-year-old girl, Dawn Ashworth, was found along Ten Pound Lane, a secluded, rural dirt road in the same area.

At first, police focused their attention on Richard Buckland, a 17-year-old with learning disabilities. Under police interrogation, Buckland confessed to killing Dawn Ashworth, however he would soon become the first person in history exonerated by DNA evidence.

English double murderer Colin Pitchfork was the first man in the world convicted of murder based on DNA evidence.

Not too long before Dawn Ashworth's body was found, a geneticist at the nearby University of Leicestershire had developed the early technology for what would come to be known as DNA profiling.

Comparing DNA samples from Buckland with semen samples of the killer taken from the victims' bodies, Sir Alec Jeffreys was able to prove that both girls had been killed by the same man – and that Richard Buckland didn't commit the murders.

From there, local police would take the unprecedented step of launching a "genetic dragnet" – soliciting thousands of DNA samples from every local man between the ages of 13 and 33. In August 1987, a woman at a local pub overheard bakery worker Ian Kelly brag that he had taken the DNA test in the name of his buddy, Colin Pitchfork.

Sure enough, when police interrogated Pitchfork, he confessed to the murders. Pitchfork's DNA matched the DNA from the killer's semen samples. Pitchfork told authorities that he had escalated from exposing himself to committing sexual assaults to rapes and then the murders. He was well on his way to becoming a serial killer.

Pitchfork was arrested on September 19, 1987, the same day police found the body of the South Side Strangler's first Richmond victim, *Style Weekly* magazine employee Debbie Davis.

Pitchfork was sentenced to life in prison in January 1988, but under the British legal system, he is now eligible for release. In November 2017 victim Lynda Mann's mother was outraged by news reports and photos of Pitchfork on an unsupervised shopping trip in downtown Bristol, the city closest to where he is imprisoned. The prison system had authorized these trips to prepare Pitchfork, who is now 57 and has legally changed his last name to Thorpe, for potential release. Denied parole in May 2018, Pitchfork will be considered for release again in 2020.

Before the advent of DNA testing, dusting for fingerprints and comparing blood types were the most scientifically advanced ways to link a criminal to a crime scene.

Police in the 1980s were still employing variations of some of the same forensic science technology that had been groundbreaking when Sir Arthur Conan Doyle was writing his Sherlock Holmes stories in the late 19th and early 20th centuries.

It is really difficult to understate how little the public knew about DNA in 1988, when Timothy Spencer, the South Side Strangler, became the first man to be sentenced to death on the basis of DNA evidence.

For most people back then, DNA was something one vaguely remembered being brought up in high school biology class. DNA wouldn't really enter the popular consciousness until five years later, in summer 1993, when director Steven Spielberg brought his latest summer blockbuster, *Jurassic Park*, to the silver screen with its fantastic premise of dinosaurs being restored to life via DNA.

By 1995, the forensic use of DNA in criminal investigations would be a widely debated point of contention during the mass-media spectacle that was the "Trial of the Century" as prosecutors introduced DNA evidence in the double-murder trial of popular Pro Football Hall of Famer-turned-actor O.J. Simpson.

And in 1998, DNA nearly led to the downfall of U.S. President Bill Clinton after his DNA was found on a semen-stained blue Gap dress that presidential paramour Monica Lewinsky had turned over to independent counsel Ken Starr. (The U.S. House of Representatives voted in December 1998 to impeach Clinton in part on grounds that he had perjured himself in federal grand jury testimony about the nature of his relationship with Lewinsky. The DNA proved he had sexual relations with Lewinsky. Clinton avoided being removed from office after he was acquitted by the U.S. Senate.)

Today, in the 21st century, virtually everyone knows about DNA. For under $100, you can buy a consumer DNA kit, swab your cheek and locate long-lost relatives – or learn if you have Neanderthals in your family tree.

But the Spencer case happened long before TV series such as *CSI: Crime Scene Investigation* or *NCIS* brought DNA and forensic science into the world's living rooms. By the time best-selling author Michael Crichton published the novel *Jurassic Park* in 1991, Timothy Spencer had already been on death row for two years.

So in fall 1987, when the New York lab Lifecodes was proselytizing for the use of DNA testing in criminal investigations, not many people would have had the vision or base knowledge to understand its potential.

But one man who did was the late Paul Ferrara, Ph.D., the director of the Virginia Department of Forensic Science.

On the heels of their success in bringing Florida serial rapist Tommie Lee Andrews to justice, Lifecodes saw Virginia's South Side Strangler investigation as a perfect opportunity to demonstrate that

DNA testing could be used to solve even the most complex homicides.

In the midst of Spencer's fall 1987 killing spree, Lifecodes offered their assistance to Ferrara, who would later cite the successful use of DNA in solving the South Side Strangler murders when he asked Virginia's state legislature to provide funding in 1989 for the state crime lab to begin performing its own DNA testing and to create the nation's first state criminal DNA database.

That would in turn help inspire the establishment in 1992 of CODIS, the FBI's national law enforcement DNA database network, which includes the DNA databases from all 50 states and Puerto Rico, as well as the federal government. (Virginia was the pilot state used in the creation of CODIS.)

As of early 2018, CODIS has produced more than 422,000 DNA matches, assisting in over 406,000 criminal investigations across the nation.

Paul Ferrara was never a household name, but he is widely recognized by his peers as one of the fathers of this country's criminal justice DNA database system. He was even profiled by legendary TV journalist Mike Wallace on the long-running national CBS news show *60 Minutes.*

Ferrara was a member of the FBI's DNA Advisory Board and the National Institute of Justice's National Commission on the Future of DNA Evidence, which was chaired by then-U.S. Attorney General Janet Reno. A former chair of the American Society of Crime Laboratory Directors/Laboratory Accreditation Board, Ferrara cofounded the Virginia Institute of Forensic Science and Medicine to train forensic scientists, toxicologists and pathologists. He also helped create a graduate program in forensic science at Virginia Commonwealth University, for which he would teach classes.

Today, in downtown Richmond, a large portrait of Ferrara hangs in the front foyer of the Paul B. Ferrara Building, the home of the Virginia Department of Forensic Science's headquarters and central laboratory.

"There's no doubts in my mind at all that the DNA results point to Timothy Spencer and no one else," Ferrara himself said about the South Side Strangler case in a 1994 interview with Richmond news radio station WRVA 1140 AM. "Everything points to a properly conducted, valid and quite well-established identification."

If a DNA databank had been in existence "at the time Spencer was committing his heinous acts," Ferrara told WRVA, "he would have been identified even earlier before some of these other crimes" because Spencer already had previous burglary convictions on his record that would have required his DNA profile to be placed in Virginia's criminal DNA database.

As director of the Virginia Department of Forensic Science, Paul Ferrara created the nation's first criminal DNA databank, which became the pilot for the FBI's national CODIS database network. (*Photo courtesy* Style Weekly)

Ferrara was a national leader in establishing scientific standards for DNA testing in criminal cases, says Kenneth E. Melson, former acting head of the ATF and a past president of the American Academy of Forensic Sciences.

"Dr. Ferrara was a tremendous influence in the forensic science world. His laboratory was just very advanced and proactive in all sorts of things," Melson says. "All I can say is, Paul Ferrara was a person who led the field and will go down in history, I think, as one of the leading individuals, both with respect to the establishment of the DNA process in their laboratory but also with respect to the quality assurance of their laboratory."

Best-selling mystery novelist and former Richmonder Patricia Cornwell praised Ferrara in a 2011 interview with Richmond television news station WTVR CBS 6: "He's one of the sort of renaissance men of forensic science," Cornwell said. "Even though his specialty is molecular biology and DNA and things like that, he knows about it all."

Virginia has collected more than 435,000 DNA samples in its criminal offender DNA database. Since its creation in 1989, the state database has returned more than 12,000 matches linking convicted criminals to other crimes. Under a pilot program established by Ferrara, the database also exonerated several prisoners who were wrongly convicted.

Earlier this year, Virginia's legislature voted to expand the state's DNA database to include samples from people convicted of misdemeanors such as trespassing and assault and battery.

If Virginia had been collecting this information in 2010, it would have likely prevented the 2014 abduction and slaying of 18-year-old University of Virginia student Hannah Graham. Her killer, Jesse Matthew Jr., was arrested for trespassing in 2010. By that point, he had already abducted, raped and murdered 20-year-old Virginia Tech student Morgan Harrington, and he had also brutally raped another woman in Northern Virginia. DNA evidence tied Matthew to all three crimes.

Privacy advocates generally oppose DNA databases, citing distrust of the government and the potential for mishandling sensitive medical information that can be uncovered from DNA results, such as what diseases a person might be at risk of getting. The ACLU of Virginia opposed adding nonviolent crimes such as trespassing to the database, says spokesman Bill Farrar.

"Certainly we agree that cold cases should be solved, especially the heinous types of crimes that the DNA databank was supposedly set up to prevent," Farrar says. "But we have really serious concerns, constitutional concerns, about privacy relating to the existing database. Because right now, we collect DNA for all felonies and a number of misdemeanors and for certain violent felonies there's not even a conviction requirement. If you get arrested for one of these crimes, your DNA is going in the database. And that's information that is the most personal, private information about an individual – that's information they might not even know about themselves about their ancestry, their lineage, about diseases they may be susceptible to, predictive behavior, so we really have serious concerns about the government taking that information at all but certainly not for minor crimes and without a conviction."

Advocates for criminal DNA databases point out that more than 60 percent of convicted criminals in the United States are likely to commit a subsequent crime. And as Spencer did, many violent criminals start out by committing lesser, nonviolent offenses, such as property theft or breaking and entering.

Furthermore, when state forensic scientists perform DNA tests in criminal investigations, they generally restrict the testing to so-called junk DNA – areas of DNA that don't hold any important information about a person. It's also against the law for forensic lab workers to release any private information about an individual's DNA outside of the database.

While criminal justice DNA databases have a proven track record for solving cold cases, one obvious drawback is that not everyone's DNA is listed in the FBI's national databank.

For instance, the DNA of Golden State Killer suspect Joseph James DeAngelo, who was arrested in April 2018, wasn't listed in any databases. A former police officer, he had no criminal record, aside from a 1979 misdemeanor shoplifting conviction that cost him his law enforcement career. DeAngelo was the first and most high-profile murder suspect located so far via a new method of cross-referencing DNA tests with genealogy databases in order to develop suspects. Investigators found DNA matches for relatives of the Golden State Killer in a public genealogy database and then researched the killer's family tree until they located DeAngelo, who lived in the correct area and matched the killer's profile.

It's expected that this genealogical database investigative approach will continue to solve more cold-case murders that had once left police stumped. In July 2018, for example, police in Indiana used this method to arrest a man who later confessed to the 1988 strangulation murder, sexual assault and kidnapping of 8-year-old April Tinsley.

At the time of the Spencer case, forensic scientists couldn't foresee the great advances in DNA testing that would take place just 30 years later.

In 1988, it could take nearly three months to make a DNA match and technicians had to be careful to protect themselves from exposure to the radioactive probes used in testing. Now the average DNA test can be done in a few days – with no radiation necessary. And there's even a new tool called the ANDE Rapid DNA system that can establish DNA matches within about an hour.

To collect a useful DNA sample in 1987, investigators needed a fairly large sample of blood, saliva or semen, about the size of a quarter or half dollar. With today's far more sensitive testing equipment, however, scientists can find DNA in specks of matter invisible to the human eye. Forensic techs can recover DNA from dried perspiration inside clothing. They can even find "Touch DNA" left behind after a person briefly touches an object such as a table or doorknob.

When Timothy Spencer was arrested, six segments of his DNA were tested – enough to calculate that the odds of any other African-American sharing his DNA signature were one in 135 million. That was at a time when the entire African-American population of the United States was only about 29 million.

Today, DNA scientists test 24 areas of a suspect's DNA. That's enough to calculate odds far greater than the entire population of planet Earth – often in the trillions. Labs use a special probability software suite called TrueAllele to calculate these mind-bendingly large numbers.

Brad Jenkins, a DNA program manager for the Virginia Department of Forensic Science, explains how it works like this:

"It's kind of like describing a car. If you said, 'I want to find a white truck' and say you name two characteristics – it's white and a truck. There might be tens of thousands of those in Virginia, where if you said it's a white truck, it's a Ford, it's an F250 and it has a leather interior, it has this type of CD player and it has whitewall tires and the first character on the license plate is an 'A,' that becomes very pinpoint in that you're able to look at all those different points to describe that car."

In the same way, Jenkins explains, "if you have [just] one or two areas of DNA, those types can be very common and you can find other people in this room [who] have that DNA type [but] if you have lots of DNA information, the 24 areas, that becomes very rare."

But without a database of known samples to compare against, that detailed suspect DNA analysis wouldn't have any value.

And that brings us back to the case of rape survivor Debbie Smith. In the aftermath of her rape, Debbie suffered years of fear and dread that her attacker might follow through on his threats and return.

"I became very suicidal," she says. "I didn't want to live. In fact, I thought that him leaving me alive, it was part of the cruel punishment, because now I had to live with this every day. I had to remember every detail every day.

Debbie Smith

"One of the things when a trauma like this happens is that you're robbed of the innocence of thinking that this can't happen to me, that it's always somebody else," she continues. "So when you're robbed of that type of innocence, now you know that you're vulnerable, so you begin to think that you're vulnerable everywhere, all the time and you never feel safe. I think, for me, fear was probably the most invasive feeling that I had."

Before the attack, she says, "I was always comfortable in my home. I always felt safe in my home ... and now this had been taken from me. I also worried constantly about my children: Where were they? I had to know where they were at every moment because I was so afraid."

In 1993 the Virginia Department of Forensic Science received the first "hit" (match) from its DNA databank. Four years later Virginia also made the first interstate hit, matching a criminal in Virginia's database to a rape committed in Florida.

And on July 26, 1995, Virginia's DNA databank returned a match for the man who raped Debbie Smith. It was only the fourth cold-crime DNA hit in the entire nation at that time – and all four matches had come out of Virginia's database.

The man who attacked Debbie was brought to justice as a direct result of the DNA database created because of the South Side Strangler case. The match had occurred after Norman Jimmerson had been imprisoned for abducting and robbing two other women in the Williamsburg, Virginia, area. His DNA profile had been entered into Virginia's state database.

"DNA had solved my case and had changed my life," Smith says. "I can't even explain to you the difference that it made in my life. It meant that my children could go off to a friend's house and I wasn't paranoid that this man was out there watching them."

At his trial, Jimmerson received two life terms plus 25 years for the rape and abduction of Debbie Smith.

That was when Debbie met Paul Ferrara.

Ferrara had come to the trial to support his staff members who were testifying about the DNA results. However, not long afterward,

Ferrara got back in touch with Debbie and asked if she would speak to a new federal commission he was serving on, the National Commission on the Future of DNA Evidence. Led by then-U.S. Attorney General Janet Reno, the commission was establishing national standards for the handling, usage and testing of forensic DNA evidence.

"And Paul thought it would be a good idea if they could find a victim who had benefited from DNA to come and speak to that commission," Smith recalls. "[Innocence Project founder and O.J. Simpson defense-team member] Barry Scheck was on the panel, there were chief justices on the panel, there were all kinds of very important people on this panel."

Smith felt overwhelmed and wasn't sure she could do it but, with the support of Ferrara and her husband, she testified before the commission. "And after I spoke," she recalls, "Paul [Ferrara] asked me if I would come and visit the lab."

During the tour, Ferrara took her into a room that had "all kinds of boxes and bags and baskets of stuff," crowded from floor to ceiling on row after row of shelving.

"What is this?" she asked, and Ferrara told her it was the backlog of evidence from rapes that the lab didn't have enough funding to get tested yet.

"And so I said, 'What can I do?'"

In 2004, after years of lobbying by Ferrara and Smith, Congress passed the Debbie Smith Act, which strengthened the national law enforcement DNA database and provided funding to reduce the backlog of untested DNA evidence. The act was reauthorized in 2008 and 2014.

Paul Ferrara "was relentless on trying to make sure that this law got passed and he was trying to make sure that people understood how important DNA is," says Debbie Smith, who today is the founder and CEO of H-E-A-R-T: Hope Exists After Rape Trauma, a Virginia-based nonprofit organization that advocates for and supports victims of rape and sexual assault.

"I know that anything that I accomplish in this life is because of Paul Ferrara and his encouragement," Debbie says. "The things that I thought that I could not do, between him and my husband, they said you *CAN* do it. It was Paul who kept telling me, 'You keep fighting this fight.' ... I saw him just about three months before he died and one of the last things he said [to me] was, 'You keep fighting for this because DNA is worth this fight.'"

Paul Ferrara died of brain cancer at age 68 in May 2011.

"I believe he's responsible for the fact that we have a DNA databank in the United States. He was so committed to this," Smith says.

"He was a special, special man and he was a fighter and when he believed in something, he was going to do whatever he could to make sure that it happened. And I am so glad that he did because, without him, I don't believe we would have had a databank. To me, that's what his legacy is."

CHAPTER 10

NIGHTMARE'S END

Over his legendary 25-year career at the FBI, special agent John Douglas helped coin the term "serial killer" and forge the investigative field of criminal behavioral profiling.

The Netflix series *Mindhunter* and a character in the Academy Award-winning 1991 film *The Silence of the Lambs* are both based on his life and work.

Douglas and his fellow special agent Robert Ressler interviewed a legion of infamous monsters such as Ted Bundy, David Berkowitz, Edmund Kemper and John Wayne Gacy, learning their methods and psychology so that law enforcement could develop valuable techniques for capturing other serial murderers.

And, nearing the end of his tenure at the FBI, Douglas had wanted to add Timothy Spencer, the South Side Strangler, to their fiendish ranks.

However, despite all of his experience and impressive credentials, Douglas' interview request was flatly refused by Spencer's attorneys.

So then Virginia State Police Senior Special Agent Larry McCann and FBI profiler Steve Mardigian decided they would try a somewhat different approach.

"Well, maybe we didn't ask," McCann says, puckishly. "I don't think we asked. Why bother to ask? We arrived unannounced at death row."

Now retired and bravely battling ALS, McCann was the first profiler in the Virginia State Police's Violent Crimes Unit. He had studied serial killers with the FBI's Behavioral Science Unit and had even interviewed the notorious serial killer John Wayne Gacy as part of his training.

"I said [to Gacy], 'Hey, tell me about all those kids you buried in your crawl space,'" McCann recalls. "He said, 'No, I didn't do that. Anybody could have done that. Anybody could have snuck up under my house and buried a kid.'

"I said, 'OK, I'll give you one [body buried under your house] but I'm not giving you 33.'"

McCann and Mardigian had worked on and off for a year plotting out how – and when – they would make their own attempt to interview Spencer and get him talking about the South Side Strangler killings.

They waited until April 1994, a week before Spencer was sentenced to die in Virginia's electric chair, before they showed up on death row at Greensville Correctional Center. A Richmond judge had just ruled against Spencer's last-ditch attempt to appeal his conviction by calling the DNA testing results into question.

"We impressed on [Spencer] immediately … that he was going to die within the week, because that's the time if you're ever going to tell a big secret, if you're ever going to tell the truth, that's when it will all come out," says McCann. "As Dante said, 'Abandon all hope, all ye who enter here.' So we waited as late as we thought prudent and that's when we went, when all hope was gone and he knew he was going to die."

Handcuffed in front, Spencer "had the longest fingers of anyone I'd ever met. Incredibly long fingers," remembers McCann. "And while I was shaking his hand as we arrived and when we departed, I thought about the necks those fingers had been around and how many terrified women those fingers had assaulted."

McCann and Mardigian sat down with Spencer and began to use all the strategies they had devised over the last year.

Spencer, McCann recalls, was "quiet, deferential. He didn't look like a monster. You wouldn't pick him out of a crowd."

McCann started the interview by telling Spencer, "You're going to die in one week and the governor will not intervene, the Supreme Court has had enough. We're not here to get any more cases solved or confessions. We just want to know how you did it [and] why you did it ... so we can stop [the next serial killer] sooner, so there aren't five or 10 victims [next time]."

Retired Virginia State Police Senior Special Agent Larry McCann interviewed Timothy Spencer on death row.

There were many answers they wanted from Spencer, the retired State Police profiler says, including, "How did you select your victims? How did you select this house? How did you get in? How did you get out? We knew what he did once he was there. But we wanted to have all the details."

McCann and Mardigian talked with Spencer for more than an hour "and he gave us nothing," says McCann. "Zero. Zip. Nothing."

Steve Mardigian says he and McCann tried every tool in their toolbox, but Spencer just wasn't having it – possibly because his lawyers were still hoping to obtain a stay of execution from the Virginia Supreme Court.

The closest they came to having a dialogue with Spencer was when McCann, who had also grown up in Arlington, talked with him about a creek they had both played in as boys.

"I said, 'You and I grew up in South Arlington right about the same time. And there's a creek. You lived on one side; I lived on the other. And as a kid, I used to go down to that creek, Four Mile Run, and splash around and throw rocks like little boys do.' And I said, 'Tim, I'll bet that one day you and I were down there at the same time. We might have been throwing rocks at the same frog at the same time in that creek. But we didn't know each other. We could have been there together.'

"And as I was going through this, he was looking at the floor. And he brought his eyes up higher and higher as I kept going through this … and he finally brought his eyes up and met mine. And then he said, 'Yeah, maybe, but I never hurt anybody.' And that's as far as he would go."

"It looked like he might at least have a conversation with Larry," Mardigian says, "but once he really understood our purpose there … he could care less whether he helped us in any capacity. He shut the interview down.

"But you take your shot. I mean, we've been in [correctional] institutions [and] we interviewed a lot of criminals that would talk to us, some very successful ones. And that's what really helped to develop the profiling field. Some do [talk] and some don't."

"We tried every one of the scenarios that we had posited for the last year," McCann says. "We tried every one: We can't save you. You're going to die. But we may be able to stop the next kid from going down this path. Tim, help us help this kid."

But, over and over again, all Spencer would say is, "Well, I don't know anything," and "I didn't hurt anybody."

"I saw him as defiant, arrogant, angry," Mardigian says. "These are the adjectives that come to mind if I recall correctly. And he was obstinate. … He was like, 'You're a cop; I don't have to talk to you.' We tried a number of different approaches to try to get the guy to open up and, you know, give us some insight into his [crimes]."

Because Spencer and his lawyers were still trying to challenge the DNA results, "he wasn't ever going to admit he did these things," says the retired FBI supervisory special agent. "But of course the evidence was so overwhelming, the blood work, the physical evidence, the DNA, there was just no way he could challenge that. And, of course, [DNA testing] was all new. No one knew about that back then. It was like science fiction stuff and it's always been tough being the first guy, you know? ... But he was the one."

In the years following Spencer's conviction, Bill and Josie Dudley, the parents of South Side Strangler victim Debbie Davis, filed a $9 million lawsuit against Offender Aid and Restoration Inc., the nonprofit organization that ran the halfway house where Timothy Spencer lived during his fall 1987 killing spree.

Spencer was in a program that was supposed to help recently paroled felons transition to leading a productive life on the outside. But, as the Dudleys' lawsuit pointed out, Spencer should never have been in the halfway house to begin with.

Timothy Spencer had been in and out of trouble with the law since age 9, when he was first arrested on charges of larceny and arson. He grew up at his grandmother's house, where he was raised with four aunts and uncles close to his age because his mother, Thelma, had moved in with a friend at an apartment complex where children weren't allowed. Spencer's father was completely absent from his life. He would visit his mother on weekends but wouldn't live with her until he was 9, after his younger brother, Travis, was born. Timothy didn't do well in school and his IQ was measured at 89, just below average. (Despite this, former Richmond homicide detective Ray Williams says that Spencer was extremely intelligent, just not book-smart. And the level of planning that went into his crimes demonstrated it, Williams says.)

As a teen, Spencer was withdrawn but handsome, attracting the attention of local girls. "My brother was dynamite gorgeous. ... Hazel eyes, that's what made him unique. They changed like the weather," Travis Spencer told a British true-crime TV show in 2009. "He was always quiet with everybody but when he and I were together, we would talk like brothers and laugh, tell each other things."

Timothy Spencer was also one of a group of kids who "terrorized the neighborhood," Travis said. "If thieving was a sport, he would have been No. 1. If you told me he stole your hubcaps, I would believe that. If you would have told me he stole your *eyebrows*, I would believe that."

Between the ages of 11 to 16, Spencer was convicted of burglary and larceny multiple times and served two stretches in juvenile correctional centers. By age 19, he was sent to the Virginia State Penitentiary for six months, again for burglary. Just one month after his release, he was promptly arrested on three new burglary charges and he was sent back to prison until March 1983 – three months before the Masked Rapist attacks began in Arlington.

After Spencer was imprisoned on breaking and entering charges in 1984, he joined in a barbaric group assault of two fellow inmates, who were threatened with rape if they reported the attack to prison officials. He also set a fire while he was in prison and attempted to set another.

Prison psychologists deemed Spencer a "potential discipline and security problem" and described him as "lazy, greedy, self-indulgent, directionless, uncooperative and unreliable."

Citing his long history of criminal offenses, the Virginia Parole Board refused to grant Spencer early release, considering it an unacceptable risk.

Timothy Spencer wasn't supposed to get out of prison until 1991, but somehow he slipped through the cracks and in early September 1987 he ended up being released to the Hospitality House halfway house in South Side Richmond, in walking distance from the homes of Debbie Davis and Dr. Susan Hellams.

Spencer didn't meet any of the parole requirements for living at the halfway house, such as being a mandatory parolee. The house also wasn't supposed to admit inmates with any history of violence.

Because residents were still considered to be in the prison system, the halfway house was supposed to monitor them and ensure they obeyed restrictions such as not possessing weapons.

But as the lawsuit notes, even though the halfway house was under contract with the state Department of Corrections, security there was nonexistent. It primarily consisted of an honor system with a sign-in sheet and head counts. In fact, the lawsuit charged that three of the four halfway house employees who were supposed to be supervising the parolees were themselves former convicted criminals – with histories of prostitution, burglary and malicious wounding. And the lawsuit further alleged that residents openly used alcohol and drugs.

Halfway house residents were supposed to obey a mandatory curfew but Spencer came and went more or less as he pleased, sometimes signing back in as late as 2:30 a.m. His bedroom window opened onto a fire escape, allowing him easy egress, and he often left to spend the night with a local girlfriend who was staying at her best friend's house about four blocks away on Bainbridge Street, according to retired Richmond homicide detective Ray Williams.

The night Timothy Spencer murdered Debbie Davis, he wasn't present for the halfway house's 7 p.m. headcount. He signed back in at 12:30 a.m., marking himself down as "late." No one asked where he'd been. The state required the halfway house to notify the Department of Corrections if an inmate was absent without leave for more than two hours. But the halfway house never filed a report.

Even more incredibly, halfway house employees *helped* Spencer break the rules. Spencer, who largely kept to himself at the halfway house, befriended a female employee there who frequently lent him her car, even though she knew he was supposed to be prohibited from driving. In exchange, Spencer performed repairs and maintenance work on the vehicle, like fixing its brakes. Police believe Spencer used the car to get back and forth from the murder of 15-year-old Diane Cho. He pulled up to the halfway house in the same sedan just moments before he was arrested.

Spencer killed his final victim, Sue Tucker, when the halfway house issued him a furlough to visit his family in Arlington over Thanksgiving weekend 1987.

Offender Aid and Restoration settled Bill and Josie Dudley's lawsuit for a sizeable but undisclosed sum and the city government shut down the halfway house.

"There was nothing, there was no amount of money that could ever adequately compensate them for the loss of their daughter and particularly for the horrendous manner of her death. She was their only child," says Richmond-area attorney and retired Chesterfield County Circuit Court Judge Michael C. Allen, who represented the Dudleys in their lawsuit.

About two weeks before he murdered Debbie Davis, Timothy Spencer was paroled to the Hospitality House halfway house in South Richmond.

"I hoped they received some manner of satisfaction at having been vindicated through the legal process to the extent they could be. Mr. Dudley did experience that. Mrs. Dudley, I think, was so grief-stricken that she was virtually a shell of a person at that time. So you know I'm not sure that the result of the lawsuit frankly gave her a great deal of solace," Allen says.

Not too long ago, Debbie's cousin Judy Fiske says, "There was talk about putting another halfway house in our neighborhood … in Westover Hills, and it was like, '*I don't think so.*'"
Judy remembers that the lawsuit against the halfway house didn't bring her aunt and uncle any peace – but they felt strongly that it had been the right thing to do.

"The lawsuit was really, really important to Bill, not for money but for, you ought not to let this stuff happen," Judy says. "He was always sad and angry. He was very angry that something like this could happen."

Bill Dudley himself told the *Richmond Times-Dispatch* in 1989 that he no longer "had the desire or heart" to make wood crafts like he once did with his daughter at his home workshop. When he became too lost in his memories of Debbie, Bill would go outside and spend time with his dogs, he said, in a futile attempt to "try to get my mind off the past."

He would die from prostate cancer in 2004, still deeply troubled and upset, having never recovered from the loss of his daughter.

"It took the peace out of his final years because he was angry and felt like something that he really loved had been taken," Judy Fiske says. "And, I mean, something he really loved *HAD* been taken away from him. He had counted on having Debbie to be around and they were best buddies. So I think he felt that big hole in his life from then on."

❖

In 1990, around the same time that the Dudleys' lawsuit was settled, and just a year after Spencer's final murder trial, a computer analyst working at the Virginia Chief Medical Examiner's Office in Richmond published her debut mystery novel.

A fictionalized version of the South Side Strangler killings, the best-selling book was called *Postmortem*. And its author, Patricia Cornwell, would ascend to literary superstardom as one of the world's most famous and successful crime and mystery writers. To date, Cornwell has sold more than 100 million copies of her books and has written 29 *New York Times* best-sellers.

Ironically, *Style Weekly* employee Debbie Davis, the Strangler's first Richmond victim, was an avid mystery reader and probably would have been a big fan of Cornwell's novels, which have gone on to influence pretty much every movie and TV show one can think of today that features medical examiners and forensics work.

Cornwell received numerous awards for *Postmortem*, which launched both her career and the series of books based around her famous heroine, Dr. Kay Scarpetta. A tough-talking, chain-smoking, brilliant chief medical examiner with a compulsion to chase the truth, Scarpetta was based on Cornwell's boss at the time, Virginia Chief Medical Examiner Dr. Marcella Fierro.

For her part, Fierro usually deflects questions about Scarpetta. Appearing on the PBS documentary series *Frontline* in 2011, Fierro quipped, "Is that me? Am I blonde, blue-eyed and 105 pounds?"

But Fierro has also said that she was impressed that her friend Cornwell, a former crime reporter for the *Charlotte Observer* newspaper in North Carolina, took the time and effort to get the science and the authentic details of forensic pathology correct in her novels.

"She was very knowledgeable about the M.E. [medical examiner] system," Fierro told *Dateline NBC* in 2015. "She would go to court with the doctors and sometimes to class just to get an idea, a feel, of what our duties really were – what was a day in the life, or many days in the life, of a working forensic pathologist. Of course, the benefit of this is it gave her books great authenticity."

And, what's more, Fierro said to *Dateline*, Cornwell "started the genre of the literature that has an emphasis on forensic pathology. And from that, of course, has been derived … *CSI*, *NCIS* and all these other programs that utilize forensic pathology as an important component of their storyline. But she was the first."

Cornwell is "a terrific writer and she really did masterful work there. [*Postmortem*] is really, really, well-written and it's just a nail-biter. What better case to prime the pump to become a crime writer? [But] the real story of what happened is even more amazing," says California-based author and attorney Paul Mones, who wrote the nonfiction book *Stalking Justice: The Dramatic True Story of the Detective Who First Used DNA Testing to Catch a Serial Killer* about the South Side Strangler killings.

Published by Simon and Schuster in 1995, *Stalking Justice* offers an in-depth account of the investigation. Told largely from the perspective of Arlington detective Joe Horgas, the book also focuses heavily on the groundbreaking forensic science used in the investigation.

Mones understands why Cornwell was drawn as he was to this epic case and to some of the larger-than-life personalities who were a part of it.

"Dr. Fierro [is] just a remarkable, remarkable person. I think anybody who's spent more than 20 minutes in her company would realize that immediately," Mones observes. "For a medical examiner, she was funny and she was sharp, and she was just a great raconteur and I think being around ... [her] would have really given you insight into this world."

Even in 2018, the South Side Strangler killings are "still a remarkable story," Mones says. "People write to me and come up to me and say, 'Wow, did all that really happen?' And I say, 'Yeah, that all really happened in Arlington and Richmond, Virginia, over 30 years ago.'"

Throughout the 1990s most Richmonders were in awe of Cornwell's meteoric rise, as her Scarpetta mystery novels continued to top the best-seller lists every year for more than a decade. But some family members of the South Side Strangler's victims, like Diane Cho's brother, Roman, found *Postmortem* disrespectful. Roman Cho still resents Cornwell profiting from a fictional story based in part on the horrific murder of his sister.

"As far as I'm concerned, she can go to hell, man. To write a book so thinly based on what happened to my sister and others so soon after it happened, I just have no kind of regard for her," Cho says. "I thought it was disgusting. It's one thing to do a book about the murders and about the South Side Strangler, but for her to make entertainment out of it, so soon after it happened, if she's going to do that, the very least she can do is explain herself. She can go to hell as far as I'm concerned.

"I mean, it's disgusting what she did. She couldn't figure out a unique plotline. She had to take that from the headlines – and take it from headlines that were so close, not only in terms of the time that lapsed since the event, but from the same city. C'mon, c'mon! Talk about, like, lack of any kind of moral compunction."

Patricia Cornwell herself spoke about her early career and *Postmortem* in 2016 during an appearance at the University of Leicester in England, which, perhaps not coincidentally, is where criminal forensic DNA testing was pioneered in the 1980s.

"I feel a tremendous responsibility for what I share with the readers and it's actually something I anguish over," Cornwell told the assembled audience. "I spend a lot of time thinking, 'How am I going to do this in a way that's not going to make it worse out there?' And that's been my anguish since the time I started writing these books.

"I almost didn't do it. Because when I got to where I was going to start *Postmortem*, and I realized that if I was ever going to make this work, I really needed to write about what I was really seeing and not make up fanciful tales about it, and I spent some real soul-searching ... [asking myself], 'But am I going to celebrate something that should be condemned?' And then I said, 'Not if you show it to people the way they need to see it.' And you're going to have to make it a little bit painful and I will do it through this character. I will make dead really dead.

"And I'm not going to trivialize [murder], but I'm also not going to be so graphic to the point that I'm almost inflicting further damage on everybody. And I'm not going to say that I haven't crossed the line sometimes. It's a tough balance. And I think sometimes I have and I wish I hadn't. But it's something that is always with me. I do weigh these things out and think about them."

By April 1994, Cornwell was months away from releasing her fifth best-selling book in the Scarpetta series, *The Body Farm*. But the serial killer who inspired her first monstrous villain wouldn't be there to see it.

Shortly before 11 p.m. on Wednesday, April 27, 1994, Timothy Wilson Spencer, the serial killer known as the South Side Strangler, was strapped into Virginia's sturdy oaken electric chair, dubbed "Old Sparky," at the maximum-security Greensville Correctional Center in Jarratt, Virginia, about 25 miles away from North Carolina. It was the last execution by electric chair before condemned prisoners would be given the choice of lethal injection. (Only one prisoner in the decades since then has chosen the chair.)

On April 27, 1994, Timothy Spencer was electrocuted in Virginia's oaken electric chair, dubbed "Old Sparky."

Spencer's mother and brother were allowed visitation rights. "I was there [his] last day on this earth, when they told us we had two minutes left to talk to him," Travis Spencer recounted on the U.K. TV series *Born to Kill?* "For you to be sitting there with a person, perfectly healthy … they damn near had to pry us apart."

None of the family members of the South Side Strangler's victims chose to attend Spencer's execution. Neither did Arlington and Richmond homicide detectives Joe Horgas and Ray Williams. Their job was to avenge the dead, not to watch another corpse get made.

"I knew it was going to happen," Horgas recalls. "I think I had an invite to be there, but what the hell do I want to go there to watch somebody die for?"

Horgas considered the execution to be "swift justice. I mean, I was kind of surprised that it happened so quick because everything I had heard was that usually U.S. death row cases go on for 20 years or more."

Williams also turned down an invitation from the prison's warden: "I have mixed emotions about the death penalty. I said, 'If anybody deserves it, he does,' but I don't consider it a personal vendetta, to be there, to watch it."

He told the warden, "We did our job. Now you do yours."

The two men who prosecuted Spencer for the murder of 15-year-old Diane Cho were present to witness Spencer's execution, however. Chesterfield County Commonwealth's Attorney Billy Davenport and his deputy prosecutor, Warren Von Schuch, believed that if they sought the death penalty against a defendant, then they had a responsibility to be there to see the sentence carried out.

Spencer, 32, walked into the death chamber wearing brand-new jeans with one pants leg cut off. That's so that an electrode could be attached to his bare calf with a brine-soaked sponge in order to increase conductivity.

Timothy W. Spencer, #131873

Timothy Spencer in 1994, not long before his execution at age 32

As he rubbed his newly shaved bald head and briefly contemplated the chair, Spencer didn't betray any signs of emotion. Fleetingly, his eyes met those of both the prosecutors after he sat down. Asked if he had any last words, the man who had viciously raped and strangled five women, and had terrorized Richmond and

Arlington over the horror-filled fall of 1987, said, "Yeah, I think ..." and then never said anything else again.

"Everybody was perched for him to say something," remembers Davenport. "I thought he was going to say 'I'm sorry' or something, but he didn't say anything."

Contrary to what one sees in the movies and on TV, there was no switch waiting to be dramatically pulled. Instead, the executioner stood in a partition behind the chair and simply pushed a button. That set off a 45-second barrage of 2,300 volts of electricity – enough to kill a horse, as one former state executioner pointed out in interview with *Richmond magazine* last year. That was followed by another cycle of electricity, intended to ensure brain death.

"You could smell the burnt flesh as you're coming out of the chamber. It actually blew a bubble up on his calf. You don't forget the smell when you come out of there," recalls Davenport, who retired in summer 2018. It was the second and final electrocution Davenport witnessed over his 30 year-career as Chesterfield's top prosecutor.

Ray Williams has his own thoughts about the last words that Spencer chose instead to take to his grave: "I think y'all got the right guy."

Officially, Timothy Spencer remained silent about his crimes right to the very end. But as it turns out, that might not be entirely true.
Jeff Everhart, Spencer's lead defense attorney for his Richmond-area murder trials, later represented a former prison guard who had gotten to know Spencer while guarding him on death row.

"He told me he had hired me because he had watched me do the Chesterfield trial. He was there at that time [because] Timothy Spencer was on death row. I told him that I had some doubts and some concerns [about Spencer's guilt] and he told me, 'Mr. Everhart, don't.'

"He said, 'I can tell you that Timothy Spencer, before he was executed, confessed to me that he had done these crimes. So don't have any doubts about what you did or didn't do and don't have any doubts about whether y'all did the right things.'

"And so, you know, to me, that meant a lot," Everhart says. "Now, is it possible he just told me that to make me feel better? I suppose it is, but that's what he said. [And] that *did* make me feel better, quite frankly."

Carl Womack, who represented Timothy Spencer in his Arlington capital murder trial for the killing of Sue Tucker, had a similar moment years later when he was representing a client who had grown up with Spencer.

"He said to me, 'Carl, I know you represented Tim Spencer. Tim and I used to pull burglaries together when we were kids. But I stopped because whenever there was a pet, Tim killed the pet.'"

That particular anecdote "stuck with me all these years," Womack says, because one of the first things he ever read about serial killers is that they're known to have an early history of torturing or killing pets and other animals.

It was "one of the things that led me to conclude that Spencer was guilty and left me with very little doubt, if any – actually I don't have much doubt at all," Womack says.

Looking back on the South Side Strangler investigation, more than the DNA, more than the fact that it was a milestone for forensic science and criminal justice, at its essence, it simply boiled down to a case of fine detective work, says *Stalking Justice* author Paul Mones.

"That is the quintessential story of American justice. It was tragic what happened to those women and somebody had to be held responsible," Mones asserts. "And Joe did not give up, even though when he initially started investigating the case, he didn't get a great reception about his theories. Ultimately everybody came around to realize that it was the same killer."

Because without Joe Horgas coming up with Timothy Spencer's name, and without Horgas connecting the Masked Rapist cases to the

South Side Strangler murders, there wouldn't have been a suspect to match to the DNA samples taken from the crime scenes.

And there most certainly would have been more murdered women, says former Arlington County prosecutor Helen Fahey.

"Joe Horgas deserves tremendous credit for what he did," Fahey says, "because if he hadn't had certain instincts, I can't imagine how long it might have taken to solve the crime and prevent further murders."

It has now been almost 35 years since Timothy Spencer murdered Carolyn Hamm. And it's going on 31 years since the South Side Strangler stalked the streets of Richmond and Arlington, Virginia, raping and strangling Debbie Dudley Davis, Dr. Susan Hellams, Diane Cho and Sue Tucker – all in just nine weeks.

Even now, in 2018, their friends and loved ones are still dealing with the aftermath of their murders. For the ones closest to them, like Diane Cho's mother and brother, or Carolyn Hamm's sister, or Sue Tucker's husband, their lives will always be marked by that horror.

All of them are glad Spencer can no longer harm anyone else. But his execution didn't bring them any closure either, says Debbie Davis' cousin, Judy Fiske. "It's like, he could be gone, [but] it's not going to bring Debbie back, so whatever," she says, bitterness evident in her voice.

Reg Tucker is a gentle soul who spent the 25 years after his wife Sue's murder plagued by overwhelming feelings of anger and grief. Contemplating Spencer's execution, however, he takes a surprisingly forgiving tone: "I wish that his spirit has found peace and that if there is such a thing as reincarnation, then I would not wish him to come back the sadist that he was. So maybe he's found peace. And I would be happy about that."

On the day Spencer was executed, Debbie Davis' mother, Josie Dudley, was interviewed by local news radio station WRVA 1140 AM. In the six years following her daughter's murder, Josie's health had declined dramatically. She was haunted by the same recurring nightmare. And she hoped Spencer's execution would finally bring her a measure of peace.

"I have been keeping a journal," she told the radio reporter. "I've been writing to Debbie every day. I hope after tonight that I can write the final chapter of her book. ...We had to go to all the trials so I know exactly what he did, they told us, and every night when I lay my head on the pillow that's [what] would come, that dream. I'd have that same dream of what he did with her in her apartment – the same dream every night, so I want to get rid of that dream."

Josie Dudley's nightmares ceased seven months later, on Christmas Day 1994, when she died from complications following heart surgery at age 68. But it was the grief that really killed her, her family says.

Thanks to the lasting legacy of the South Side Strangler case, more and more monsters like the Golden State Killer are being brought to justice by DNA testing. And due to DNA databanks and advances in forensic science, many violent offenders are being caught before they can escalate into becoming serial killers.

And, now, some nightmares will never have the chance to begin.

APPENDIX A: MAPS

South Side Strangler sites in Richmond, Virginia

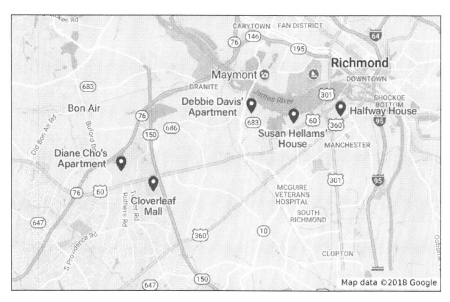

Arlington, Virginia locations

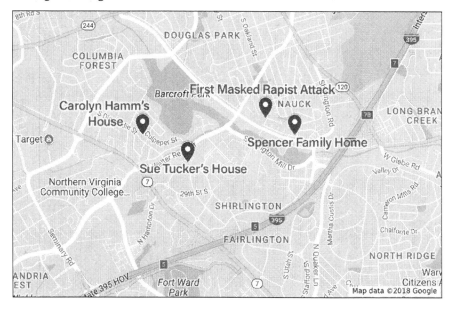

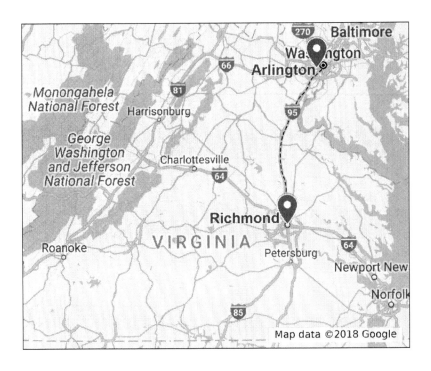

APPENDIX B: TIMELINE

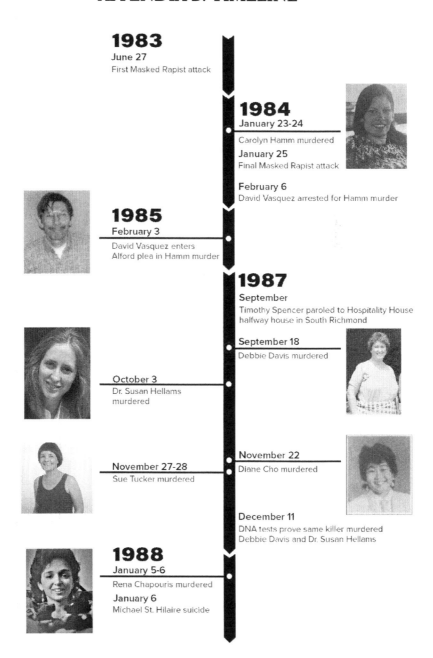

1983
June 27
First Masked Rapist attack

1984
January 23-24
Carolyn Hamm murdered

January 25
Final Masked Rapist attack

February 6
David Vasquez arrested for Hamm murder

1985
February 3
David Vasquez enters
Alford plea in Hamm murder

1987
September
Timothy Spencer paroled to Hospitality House
halfway house in South Richmond

September 18
Debbie Davis murdered

October 3
Dr. Susan Hellams
murdered

November 22
Diane Cho murdered

November 27-28
Sue Tucker murdered

December 11
DNA tests prove same killer murdered
Debbie Davis and Dr. Susan Hellams

1988
January 5-6
Rena Chapouris murdered
January 6
Michael St. Hilaire suicide

1988 cont.

January 20
Spencer indicted and arrested for Tucker murder

February 3
Glenn Williams suicide

March 16
DNA matches link Spencer to murders of Davis, Hellams and Tucker

July 15
Spencer found guilty of capital murder of Sue Tucker

September 22
Spencer found guilty of capital murder of Debbie Davis

November 2
Spencer receives 1st death sentence

November 4
Spencer receives 2nd death sentence

1989

January 4
Vasquez pardoned, released after 5 years in prison

January 20
Spencer found guilty of capital murder of Dr. Susan Hellams

February 27
Spencer receives 3rd death sentence

May 12
Spencer found guilty of capital murder of Diane Cho

June 16
Spencer receives 4th and final death sentence

1990

January 9
Publication of Patricia Cornwell's first novel, *Postmortem*

1994

April 27
Execution of Timothy Spencer

APPENDIX C: RAY WILLIAMS INTERVIEW

This interview with retired Richmond Police homicide detective Ray Williams and *Style Weekly* founder Lorna Wyckoff took place at the *Southern Nightmare* Live event at Virginia Commonwealth University in May 2018.

Richard Foster (RF): Ray, right before these killings started, you had a pretty remarkable opportunity that prepared you for what was going to happen. You were one of 50 detectives who were chosen for a special honor. Can you tell me about that?

Ray Williams (RW): One detective from each state was chosen to attend the Behavioral Science Unit in Quantico. I attended class for 10 months and they had some of the actual detectives that worked on the John Wayne Gacy case. ... I was not familiar with serial killers. That was a great school. You stayed up there weeks and came home weekends and two weekends after I finished that course was when this first murder happened.

RF: So he spent 10 months studying about serial killers. Two weeks later, first serial killer of his career. And if any of you have watched the Netflix series *Mindhunter*, anybody familiar with that one? John Douglas, Robert Ressler, yeah? Ray interacted with those guys. And also all the case files they mentioned, like Edmund Kemper and those folks, you guys studied those.

RW: And once you go through a class like that, you remember every detail. I mean Gacy, he got, he just buried kids under his crawl space. He got pictures taken with [First Lady] Rosalynn Carter during a political campaign. He was a clown. So you know, you can be walking down the street, you're not going to know who a serial killer is.

RF: But I think clown ... clown is a good indication. [*laughter from audience*] I think that's a safe one. Alright so, Lorna, at the time of the murders, Debbie Davis had been working as your accounts manager at *Style Weekly* for two years. So tell us a little bit about Debbie. What do you remember about Debbie?

Lorna Wyckoff (LW): Debbie was wonderful. Everybody loved Debbie. Debbie was the kind of employee who was just dedicated and happy and loved her friends and had bowls of candy on her desk. If there was going to be a Christmas party or a tree or a this or that, you'd go to Debbie and she would be the person who would take care of that. I loved working with her. One of the things that she did for us was collect our accounts and you know we were young and didn't really know what we were doing so it was very easy for people not to pay their bills. And, you know, collecting bills from restaurateurs is not the easiest thing in the world. Some of us were known to walk into places and pick up cash registers and you'd just walk out. But Debbie loved calling these people in the sweetest way and collecting money and working out credit plans and would come back deliriously happy that she had all these various successes and so we started talking about paying her a commission. And so she could take the most mundane things and make them wonderful.

RF: And now an interesting fact: Lorna and Ray worked very closely together following the murder. I believe this is the case, the two of you have not seen each other in 30 years. Tonight is the first time I think in 30 years the two of them have seen each other.

LW: [*To Ray*] Although I did see you in some nightmares. [*laughter from audience*]

RF: So Lorna, tell us about the way you met Ray.

LW: It was a Saturday morning in September and we lived on Monument Avenue. My husband and I were going to get our daughter and the doorbell rang and two men in suits were standing out there and walked in the door and just told us, Did Debbie Dudley Davis work for us? Yes. And after that ... I think I fainted early on. ... And it was very clear and obvious at the outset that this appeared to be something that might have been about this scrappy young paper that sometimes said rude things about people and we had [food] reviewers who would write for us, like my favorite [review] was the coffee tasted like someone had poured it through a sneaker. And then two days later the restaurant owner would be on our doorstep, so ...

RF: This was before Starbucks.

LW: And so it wasn't unusual that we could write something and irritate someone, though we certainly never intended to. Never wrote anything that we thought would be consequential, so when Ray and his partner were investigating, the first thing they did was to go down to the *Style* offices and rifle through everything, and then there was a lot of investigation about what we wrote and who said what and I understand that there was some thought that [the murder] was intended for me for a while.

RF: Let's go ahead and switch to that, Ray. So initially you guys were thinking that Debbie's murder might have been a case of mistaken identity.

RW: Yeah because one thing for a homicide investigation you got to find out everything about the victim and the attack. Well we couldn't really develop anything. ... We knew it was tough when I first walked into the scene. We knew we had a special case.

RF: Let's talk about that, so you were downtown at Seventh and Main, Eighth and Main, when you got the call that Saturday morning and you went to Debbie Davis's apartment and she lived at the time right off of Forest Hill Avenue.

RW: [*Gives exact street address and apartment number for Debbie Davis*]

RF: That is the memory of a homicide detective. That's pretty impressive. And what did you find when you got into her apartment?

RW: When I got there, the uniformed officers are trained to secure the scene and then don't touch anything, [get] back out. [The responding officer] finally got the next-door neighbor; he got a key from her and walked in and walked down, there's a living room, short hallway, bathroom and here was the bedroom on the left at the end of the hallway...

RF: And then you found, you saw a body?

RW: Yes. I saw a body laying across the bed, head hanging off, with hands tied behind her back and two socks tied around her neck with a 15-inch extension pipe from the vacuum cleaner and turned and twisted. [*audience gasps*]

RF: It had been used like a tourniquet.

RW: Exactly what it was. We found out with the medical examiner with each victim, he was taking two three hours to kill them.

RF: And Ray, what are we looking at here? [*Looks at image from PowerPoint slideshow projected on screen*]

RW: This is the kitchen window to Debbie's apartment. Below that ... [outside] he had stolen a rocking chair from a block up from an old folks' home and he stood on there and ... opened the window. Nothing on the counter or anything was disturbed so we knew at that point, my partner and I knew that we were dealing with someone agile and probably young and we felt like he'd already gained entry to the house before she got home. ... I can actually say in all the homicides I was investigating ... I was in [the police] academy in 1971 and I made detective and went right to homicide and we only had four homicide detectives and [by 1987] I'd probably worked 50 to 75 homicides. And I knew when I walked in the bedroom that we were in trouble. I told Glenn, my partner, I said, "This is scary. This is unusual." We sat and processed the scene for five days, recovered one hair from the bed sheet. No fingerprints, no nothing.

RF: No witnesses.

RW: No witnesses. ... He never made any noise and we figured that he probably wore a mask and a jumpsuit. ... We got a call to ... Forest Hill Avenue, on a car running, and it had been running all night. Guy gets home at 2 o'clock at night and the Renault is running out front, so we ran a check on it and that led back to Debbie Davis. Well, during one of the interviews with the suspect, I asked him could he drive a straight-drive transmission. No. Well, see, Forest Hill Avenue is a straight thoroughfare all the way through South Side. ... We feel like that he left, took the car, he couldn't shift gears so he left it [with] the battery running and it ran from 2 o'clock till 10 o'clock, when the officer found it.

RF: We know that the last people Debbie talked to were her parents. She spoke to them from roughly 8:30 p.m. that Friday evening to around 9:30 p.m. Debbie needed to get her gallbladder out soon. She was having some medical issues and was talking with her parents about coming back home to the Lynchburg area where she's from so they could take care of her while she would get surgery.

189

That was the last time her parents spoke with her. Ray, while Debbie was having this phone conversation with her parents, where was the South Side Strangler?

RW: We feel like he was in the closet. [*audience gasps*] Because she came from her bedroom, she had glasses on and [her] toothbrush so we think she walked across the hallway, came out and he grabbed her and [her] glasses came off and [she dropped her] toothbrush. He put duct tape over her mouth and then he ... he always carried a kit. It's called a murder kit. But we never found the murder kit. They also take souvenirs. Never found a souvenir. But we knew that we were in trouble with this. You know, your run-of-the-mill homicide, we knew it wouldn't be that.

RF: And Lorna what was it like at *Style* after the murder?

LW: It's hard to describe. We spent the weekend calling everyone and going ... Lots of us lived in the Fan and so there was a lot of walking and congregating and hugging and crying and all of that. And I remember Monday morning we called [the Rev.] Ben Campbell, who's now at Richmond Hill and he was with St. Paul's at the time, to come and he did a session for us and he gathered us all together and we all talked about Debbie and people were just ... sad.

At the time we knew our friend had been killed. We knew none of the details, we didn't know it was the South Side Strangler, we didn't know that this was a serial killer. We just felt the loss of this dear friend. Two weeks later and those two weeks were disturbing and upsetting with police all over the place and all that. Two weeks later when Dr. Hellams was murdered, we knew that it wasn't particular about *Style* or me or anyone else in the office but the fear that escalated.

So we were also in this odd position of covering it as well. And some people, lots of people were working on it and trying to figure out how to cover it and how not to be part of the story. I had lots of details that I would furnish to our reporter and certainly wanted to.

But that began the beginning of this huge fear around the city, this paranoid sense of, particularly women, who were trying to protect themselves and being frightened to go out alone and television would do these little stories about women, if you're afraid, nail your windows shut. And there was that whole sort of mentality of fear. And it went on for months. It went on for a long time.

RF: Ray, Lorna brought up Dr. Hellams. So two weeks after Debbie Davis ...

RW: Two weeks to the day. It was Saturday.

RF: Two weeks later, Dr. Hellams' murder is called in. And you go in, you see a virtually identical M.O. What did you say to your partner, Glenn?

RW: I told Glenn, we're looking for the same son of a bitch that killed Debbie Davis.

RF: And you knew at that point ...

RW: We knew ... same M.O. but he cut the screen upstairs [at Hellams' home and] broke in and was probably in her closet when she got home. ... She's wearing a red dress and double-tie belt. He put both belts around her neck and stood on her back and pulled it. It would keep rendering [her] unconscious. He'd wait 'til she came back. He'd rape her and he'd leave pure semen samples all over the room.

RF: Hence the DNA?

RW: Yes.

APPENDIX D: JOE HORGAS INTERVIEW

This interview with retired Arlington County Police homicide detective Joe Horgas was conducted in February 2018.

Richard Foster (RF): You were facing a pretty tough case here. You had no fingerprints right? No witnesses? How did you handle that?

Joe Horgas (JH): Well, in my mind, first thing I got to do is talk to David Vasquez. And I don't know if it was one or two days after or I don't even know how soon. It was pretty quick. I believe within one or two days after the body was found, probably two days I'm guessing, maybe three days. I hooked up with one of the lawyers for Vasquez. He had two lawyers and I hooked up with one of them and he agreed to go with me down to the penitentiary to talk to Vasquez and I've done a lot of interviewing, interrogation, and he just didn't act like he even knew anything about the case. He just didn't come across as having done it. We interviewed him for, I don't know, I think we were in the warden's office at the penitentiary. And it seemed like we talked for an hour, an hour and a half, and it was like spinning your wheels and not going anywhere. He just didn't know anything.

RF: Describe David Vasquez. What was he like, what did he look like? Tell me about him.

JH: Well, I mean, I felt sorry for him. I mean, he basically said that he had been raped in there. I mean he had every incentive to get the hell out of prison. He was sad, very sad case. At the time I didn't know that he had such a low IQ. He was very meek kind of guy.

RF: Was he childlike?

JH: No, no, but sad, sad, almost pathetic. He flat-out told us that he had been raped in there and he was scared shitless and all this stuff. And I already had the blessing of the commonwealth attorney's office to offer him basically his freedom if he would tell us who actually killed Carolyn Hamm. But he just didn't know anything.

RF: So when you talked to him, you were pretty much convinced that there was an innocent man in prison?

JH: Yeah. It was a touchy subject because, keep in mind, I'm working with the guys that put him away. So, I mean, I never, the best of my recollection, I never come right out and said I think David Vasquez was innocent, but at the same time you can add two and two together. When I came up with this Masked Rapist as the killer, you know how to add two and two [and] you know David Vasquez has to be innocent if my theory is correct. There was some hostility from my people only because they felt like I was saying Vasquez was innocent and, I mean, I did, by saying this guy's the killer.

RF: When did you start to put together the theory that the serial rapes and the Hamm and Tucker murders were all committed by the same person?

JH: Well, hell, if you want to be honest about it, I started putting that together back when I came back from Pennsylvania back when Carolyn Hamm had been killed. I mean, that was always in the back of my mind. Only, it kind of went away after they locked up David Vasquez. And, you know, everything stopped. So everybody assumes, well, you know we've got the right guy. I mean, you understand, everything stopped once they locked up Vasquez, everything stopped.

When I came back from interviewing Vasquez in my mind I'm pulling all these rape cases, I'm going to start looking for clues.

And so at the time, Mike Hill was my partner. I don't even remember how we started the little task force. They gave us two guys from the sex squad. One went with Hill and the other one went with me.

Me and I think it was Chapman were pulling all the rape cases to get all the evidence and everything from them. What the hell were the other two on? I think they were maybe getting burglaries and stuff like that. But we were going in two different directions.

My investigation was to put together all the rape cases, check all the evidence. And that's what I did.

I actually had an easel set up that I had put all the similarities on it.

And we're approaching Christmas and we're approaching the meeting with the FBI because that's the most significant part of this investigation.

RF: And why is that?

JH: Because they're the ones that told me how to find who the suspect is.

RF: Why was the FBI brought in?

JH: Well, because No. 1, they had already done some kind of a profile on the Richmond cases and their profile was a white male. So the FBI behavioral unit, they had profiled a white male down in Richmond and there was a doctor down in Richmond named

Dr. [Park] Dietz who wrote an article and they had an article in the newspaper down there quoting him that one thing's for sure, this is definitely a white guy you're looking for. Black people don't do serial murders or something like that.

So I had this big scenario and I wanted some input from the [FBI] Behavioral Science Unit. And so I called them up and I basically told them I think you're making the wrong profile. You got to see what I have and so we set up a date.

And it was either one or two days after Christmas 1987 that they came to the office

RF: How did the meeting go?

JH: Well, like I said, I had everything laid out. I had photos, I had everything. I had the reports from each case. I broke everything down, all the similarities and everything. They spent about an hour or two looking over everything and the short story is they ended up agreeing with me that they think this Masked Rapist is the killer and they said, we're going to go one step further: If this first case that you have, the one where he found the woman at the phone booth and made her drive him down to Green Valley, if that's the first case, then where he took her to, he's going to live within a two-block area of where he took her to. If this is his first case, he wants to make sure he's going to get away and where but his backyard pretty much can he get away? He's sure he can get away and so that little bit of information is what ended up cracking the case eventually. It wasn't that quick. But it happened.

RF: How did you come up with Timothy Spencer's name?

JH: I mean, I was asking everybody for anybody to come up with the name of anybody from that area that they knew, that we could look at, to compare. We pulled probation, parole records looking for anybody that got out of prison that would have lived in that area. We also asked Richmond to do the same stuff. But we're looking, and whether he lived in that area or not, from the probation and parole stuff, we're looking for someone who got locked up after Carolyn Hamm was killed and who was out prior to [Debbie] Davis being killed down in Richmond. This went on for several weeks, I believe. And there came a time when Mike Hill and I were sitting in the conference room one afternoon and, I mean, I've got to tell you, Green Valley was my expertise. I used to catch all the robberies and everything from down there. It was my forte, I guess. I mean, I was just good with the people down there.

[And the name] Timmy popped in my mind, only I couldn't remember his [last] name. All I could remember was Timmy. All I could remember was Timmy.

And then this one day Mike Hill and I are in the conference room. We're comparing names against each other and all of a sudden Timmy Spencer's name popped in my head. I finally remembered. And that doesn't mean it's him; it just means it's another [name] to put into the pile. But then when we ran him in the computer and when we found out that he was arrested in Alexandria for a burglary right after Carolyn Hamm was killed, it got our interest. So Mike went over to Alexandria and he pulled the arrest records, all the incident reports and everything. And what happened over there was Timmy was seen coming out of one house and going into the other house. Neighbors saw him coming out as he had broken into one house and he was getting ready to go into the other house when they called the police. The police caught him red-handed.

And so when you look at the incident report and you see the evidence they had there, I mean, the [Masked] Rapist, he always had something on his hands. Well, Timmy's socks were not on his feet. No. 1, he had Puma sneakers on. And in one case on Greenbrier Street, he raped a lady and I think her husband came from work or something in the early stages maybe in August or something of '83 and he escaped by jumping out the bedroom window or bathroom, some window. But there was a Puma sneaker track left. He's wearing Puma sneakers, his socks are not on his feet, they're in his pockets, he's wearing a tan Eisenhower jacket, which is what the rape victims describe the Masked Rapist as wearing. So this was all deserving of more looking into.

So we called probation parole to find out where he's at. Well, turns out he's still in the prison system but he's in a halfway house down in Richmond and then we go down to Richmond and we go to the halfway house and we find out that he signed himself out for every murder down there. And he got a furlough to come up to Arlington for the Susan Tucker murder.

So everything just seems to fit the puzzle. The pieces are all coming together now.

RF: You knew you had him.

JH: I knew I had him, but there were still a lot of people who didn't. [*laughs*]

RF: Let's talk about that. You had realized this was connected to the Richmond cases by that point?

JH: Yeah, I'm guessing, oh, maybe after I came back from talking to Vasquez. My sergeant had a teletype laying on my desk and it was from Richmond and I don't [remember] which [murder] it was, but it was with the M.O. and everything. So I called down there and I talked to Glenn Williams. We compared cases and we decided we got to get together and the next morning Chuck Shelton and I drove down to Richmond to attend their ... they had a weekly meeting with their prosecutor, Von Schuch. So we went down for the meeting the next day and we brought all our pictures and they had all their pictures and we compared it. It didn't take much of a brain to see that everything's done by the same guy.

RF: Did Richmond buy into your theory that the Richmond murders were connected to Arlington?

JH: I think they did. Even though it's 100 miles apart, you know what are the odds that there's a guy killing our women this way and he's killing this woman up in Arlington the same way? I think they were onboard on that. I'm going from memory here. ... [Also] I believe all these cases had the same blood typing. I'm not 100 percent sure on that but I'm pretty sure we [already] had the blood typing.

RF: When you figured out this was a serial killer, what did you think?

JH: I was not approaching it any differently. When you're putting the puzzle together, you just got to gather all of the pieces. And so I just basically gathered Richmond's pieces of the puzzle, if you will, to put into the big puzzle. I think [Arlington Commonwealth's Attorney] Helen [Fahey] was more into the bigness of this than I was. I mean, I just wanted to catch my guy. I wasn't thinking of, you know, big-time serial killer or history being made or anything like that. In fact, even at the time, until it came time to utilize DNA, I wasn't even thinking about DNA.

RF: What did Richmond think when you were going to arrest Spencer?

JH: Richmond was in on the arrest, you know that? We arrested him in Richmond. ... Of the two Williams Boys, Glenn was the nice one. Ray's just an egotistical big shot. I mean he just dwells on ego. Glenn was a down-to-earth, common guy.

RF: Tell me about arresting Timothy Spencer.

JH: So what happened is Spencer is the suspect and we let Richmond know that Spencer's our suspect. We let them know everything, I told you, about what he was wearing at the time he was picked up for the burglary, the fact that he checked himself out of the halfway house and all that stuff. So they watch him for a week. They surveil him for a week, and they let us know we don't think this is the right guy. So we're dropping the surveillance. Well, Helen panicked and we had a big meeting. And I think it was on a Friday. So she wanted me to start doing a search warrant and the game plan was to get a search warrant to get [Spencer's] blood to check it against DNA so I was in there on a Saturday in the conference room. And you know how long the search warrants going to be, I mean it's got to be everything I've told you –you've got to put all the cases together. You've got to [assemble] all the evidence from each case, then you've got to tie in the burglary and Alexandria and everything he was wearing. You know, you've got to tie all this stuff in [and] it's going to be very lengthy.

So I was in there working on that and the conference door was open and Helen [Fahey] walked by and I said, "Hey, what are you doing here today?" And she said, "I'm here because we're preparing for grand jury Monday." I said, "Hey, that's nothing but a probable cause hearing right?" She said yeah. I said, "Why don't you save me a lot of work and why don't we just go directly to the grand jury and we don't have to do a search warrant?" She said, "Let me think about that." So she came back by an hour or two later and she says, "You're on for Monday," so that's what happened. Monday, I went to the grand jury and I basically told them the same story I'm telling you and they indicted him and that night we went down to Richmond to lock up Spencer.

We had to wait for him to come home. He was at work or something. I don't know where he was, but I think we knew what time he got home or something. Me, Mike Hill [and] Henry

Trumbull from Arlington went to Richmond to meet with the Williams Boys. And I don't even know how many people were involved, but I know we were outside the halfway house waiting for him to come home. And when he comes home; short story is, he walks into the halfway house, he's checking in, and about the same time he's checking in, we're there to arrest him.

Now I didn't tell him he was under arrest for murder. I told him he was under arrest for burglary because burglary was one of the indictments. Then we handcuffed him and basically put him on ice. And I think somehow I think he wanted something from upstairs in his room. I forget – I think we went upstairs. We took him up to his room. I don't remember. It's all vague but I know Trumbull drove the car with me and Spencer in the back seat going back to Arlington.

RF: Right. And that's when he talked to you?

JH: I don't remember much. I mean, I talked to him when we got to Arlington also and I'm not sure I remember what was talked about in the car versus what was talked about in the interview room, but I know there came a time where he basically consented to have blood taken from him for DNA purposes. … Spencer didn't think they could get his [DNA]. … He knew he didn't cut himself. So that's why he didn't hesitate on giving his blood

RF: How did Spencer react when you arrested him?

JH: He was kind of smug. I mean, believe me, I worked on him, you know? I mean, most of my cases, I get confessions. I didn't get one in this case. Richmond came up and they worked on him a couple of days later. I remember that they came up to talk to him. They didn't get anywhere with him.

APPENDIX E: DR. MARCELLA FIERRO INTERVIEW

This interview with retired Virginia Chief Medical Examiner Dr. Marcella Fierro, M.D., was conducted in November 2017.

Richard Foster (RF): What do you remember about the South Side Strangler murder cases?

Dr. Marcello Fierro (MF): I did some [of the] cases [Dr. Susan Hellams and Diane Cho] … I just remember that they were really terrible, cruel cases and that I think the police figured out that most of these occurred on a Friday night. We were very concerned that something bad would happen on a Friday night. The whole city was just on edge. And I think it wasn't really until the police and the lab made the connections between the Northern Virginia homicides and the Richmond homicides that we actually got a full picture of what was going on.

RF: When DNA linked the homicides and proved they were committed by the same perpetrator?

MF: DNA was just coming online and it took a very long time to do the testing and it took a lot of special training. I think it took months to a year to transfer the technology from New York to Virginia, but once they got it going, it worked. It took a long time and the lab worked hard. We didn't extract the DNA. What we did was examine each of the victims for evidence of sexual assault and then recover from the body the material that could be used to extract DNA. The actual performance of the DNA testing [in the South Side

Strangler cases] was [done] in the [New York Lifecodes] laboratory. The collection of the material to be tested was collected by the medical examiner. There's a standard procedure for examining victims of sexual assault, whether they're male or female, and that involves looking and swabbing various body surfaces and orifices and then maintaining that material safely and under the proper conditions so that the laboratory can use it to recover DNA. Using sexual assault examination procedures, we were able to recover from the victims the seminal fluid that was tested [for DNA].

RF: What do you recall from the case of Dr. Susan Hellams?

MF: It was awfully cruel. I mean, her home was invaded and she was killed in her own place and very cruelly strangled.

RF: What do you do when you're examining victims of murders such as these?

MF: Well, when you're doing medical legal death investigations, you need to do a couple things: First is, you have to get some kind of picture of what the scene was all about and see what conclusions you can draw – what conclusions can be made [from] the physical examination of the body. That's part of it and the other part, of course, is the autopsy, which gives you the actual physical findings and any medical evidence that might be present. And third would be the correlation of those two sources of information to see what you can develop that would be helpful to law enforcement.

RF: I know that you've said to me in the past that in your personal view, you see yourself as an advocate for the victims, that you give them a voice.

MF: Somebody has to speak for the victim, at least in terms of what their injuries really were and what evidence could be recovered, otherwise neither the police nor the courts nor the family have valid scientific information upon which to make a judgment

RF: You are a former president of the National Association of Medical Examiners (NAME) and you've been a leading national voice for establishing standards for medical examiners and advocating that more states adopt laws requiring death investigators to possess medical degrees and professional credentials.

MF: Only half the states are covered by medical examiner systems, maybe less. Other states have coroner systems — coroner systems may or may not require credentialing of the people who are coroners. I mean, in some states you [only] have to be 18 and free of a felony. And so these are people who are charged with death investigation and that doesn't work, so many states don't have adequate coverage. There should be standards for death investigations. There should be standards for coroners and autopsy services.

RF: You're also known for looking for signs of sexual assault in death cases when others might have missed it.

MF: I was very finicky about that. I did not make any assumptions that sexual assault did not occur. ... We know that half of women who are sexually assaulted don't show any injury. Women who are sexually active may not show much injury, if any, so it's not something that appears foremost in some people's minds but being a woman and recognizing that information from the literature, that you could certainly have sexual assault without injury, made me more cognizant of the fact that it could occur, so I would test for it more often.

RF: You were also known for driving your beat-up, old 1975 Oldsmobile station wagon to murder scenes.

MF: That I did, yes I did. I drove it until it froze at the intersection of River Road and Cary Street and stopped traffic in the middle of the rush [hour] and it died deader than a doornail. We had to get a new car. I always drive my cars into the ground. Once it's paid for, man, I drive that car right until it dies.

RF: You're also known for making extra effort to get to crime scenes.

MF: My kids told me one day, "Gee, Ma, we saw up your skirt." [*laughing*] … In those days, you know, women didn't wear pants. And so I'm climbing up this ravine and, of course, [TV news reporters are] shooting like crazy with their cameras and that made the 6 o'clock news, which my children saw. Oh lord.

RF: Was it required to visit the scene in person or did you believe in seeing the body in context of the crime scene or where it was found?

MF: Oh I think medical examiners … like very much to see the body in context. The scene is very helpful in telling you what occurred and for getting an idea of what you should be looking for as physical evidence on the body. You saw a kitting needle at the scene? Well, you should look and see if there are any knitting needle injuries or if something could be misinterpreted as a knitting needle injury – in other words, you don't want to call it a gunshot.

RF: Did you go to the South Side Strangler murder scenes?

MF: No, I don't believe I went to those scenes. … I guess I was not on call that night and the bodies were ordered in.

RF: Did you ask to see photos of the murder scene?

MF: Yes, yes, I always look at the scene photographs. ... And you also want to talk with the police officers who took the photographs so they can interpret anything you can't figure out or that isn't apparent. They often have a great deal more information to add to the photographs.

RF: I remember that you're also an avid traveler in your spare time. Where have you been lately?

MF: Where were we last? Venice and the Croatian coast, the Dalmatian coast. ... Save your money. I used to tell people in my office that if you want to travel, save your lunch money. Save your $6 [every day] – put that $30 [a week] in a pot and at the end of the year you can go to Bermuda.

RF: I know you've been to Japan, Italy, France, England. What's the most exciting place you've been?

MF: The most exotic place is China – we've been twice. It's a marvelous place to visit – extraordinary, very different culture, very different art, very different architecture. It's a fabulous place to visit. You have to take a guided tour because all the signs are in Chinese and the distances are huge. You have to fly from place to place

RF: I know you shared being a smoker with your alter ego, Dr. Kay Scarpetta from your friend Patricia Cornwell's murder mystery novels. But she gave it up. Have you?

MF: I may be the last living physician smoker, but I am trying to quit and I would tell anybody who can quit, quit – it will kill you.

RF: Was it tough seeing so much cruelty and horror in your work?

MF: It's a dark place for these folks – all those victims. If you sat every day and said help me remember my cases, you would be so depressed, you would go sit and a corner and you'd never come out. You see so much pain and suffering. You know that these people suffered so you do what you can for them at the time and then you try and live your life.

RF: Well, I know you called them your patients and that you thought of them that way.

MF: They _were_ my patients. The only thing I didn't do that other doctors do is I didn't listen to their chest. I took [their medical] history, I did a physical examination, requested laboratory studies, made diagnoses. I do what doctors do.

RF: And also you gave them their dignity. They're in a position that they would never have wanted anyone else to see them in, they're naked and whatever happened to them is exposed to the world as well.

MF: They do deserve their dignity in death. It was my job to make sure they had it. By treating them like I would treat a living person.

RF: I also remember firsthand that, unlike coroners or medical examiners in other states, you wouldn't allow media to witness you working.

MF: We didn't have that kind of open-door policy. Attendance at autopsies was restricted to other physicians, police officers investigating the case, attorneys representing the either commonwealth or … a defense lawyer … and trainees. We were very tight on our restrictions. We didn't think this was a spectator sport. We did not think that autopsies were a spectator sport.

RF: Did you come into contact with the victims' families much?

MF: All the time – families wanted to know what happened. We talked to families all the time. They would call and ask what happened — and we would say, well, he was in a motor vehicle accident. ... They would want to know if he suffered, that sort of thing, and we would tell them the truth.

RF: You never lied about that to make them feel better?

MF: You can't lie – if we didn't think [the victim was] aware, we said so. If a motor vehicle [fatality victim] has severe head injuries, it's pretty clear they were not aware.

RF: And you saw death in many forms, of course. You would see corpses from all ages, from probably birth to elder age and every conceivable type of mishap or murder from being burned, drowned, probably all kinds of things, – every conceivable mishap or murder, yes?

MF: Skeletonized too.

RF: That makes cause of death a lot harder to determine, doesn't it?

MF: Sometimes, yes. Sometimes it's apparent, sometimes it isn't.

RF: Have they ever called you in on any archaeological cases?

MF: Occasionally, we'd get calls to establish archeological cases and to establish that they were in fact archaeological and not of forensic significance. I remember, the most excellent case [example]: Very early in my career they were building the Downtown Expressway and a bulldozer or backhoe or whatever machine sliced off a section of earth and found a skeleton. Well, I went out there, hotfooted out there, and it turned out to be an Indian burial — so it was not of forensic significance but was of interest in terms of archeology and history of the region. So once I established this was not a case for the medical examiner, it was left then for the archaeologists and anthropologists to figure it out.

RF: Was there any urgency in the South Side Strangler murders? Were the police trying to get the information quicker than usual? Or asking you to examine the bodies quicker?

MF: We would like to examine the body and recover the evidence as soon as it is practical. …You would try to get to that case first. … You just want to get the evidence to the police as quickly as possible so they can submit it to the lab as quickly as possible. … I don't think it's a matter of pressure. It's a matter of being sure you put into practice the procedures that you know need to be done … expeditiously. It doesn't do any good to pressure the medical examiner because the result will be the same whether it's an urgent case or a non-urgent case. You bring to each case all of the experience and knowledge that you know.

RF: When you're working on a serial killing, are there things you might find in your examination that would help inform their profile of the killer?

MF: Sometimes you can help link cases if they're from different jurisdictions. For example, if there's a Richmond case and then a Henrico case and a Chesterfield case that you see similarities in, then you will alert those officers that they might have a linkage. … Sometimes you can see the pattern before they do.

APPENDIX F: LARRY MCCANN INTERVIEW

This interview with retired Virginia State Police Senior Special Agent Larry McCann took place at the *Southern Nightmare* Live event at Virginia Commonwealth University in May 2018.

Richard Foster (RF): You are one of the people who came face-to-face with the South Side Strangler and you spent some time with him. Can you tell me what you remember from meeting him? What sort of impression did he make on you?

Larry McCann (LM): Well, unlike Ray [Williams], I wasn't part of the initial investigation that brought him down. I was just on the edges of that. But when he was on death row in Virginia, I went to see him. In Dante's *Inferno*, as you go through the gate to Hell, there's a sign: "Abandon hope all ye who enter," and if you want to find out the truth from a violent offender, the best time to talk to him is when he has abandoned all hope, so for a year, an FBI agent and I looked into his life, his victims, the way he worked, and we went to him a week before his execution.

The first thing I noticed was his fingers. When I shook his hand, he had the longest fingers I had ever seen and I had to think at that moment how many necks had those fingers been around and I said, first thing after we shook hands, told him who we were and I said, "You're going to die in one week and you know the governor will not intervene, the Supreme Court has had enough. We're not here to get any more cases solved or confessions. We just want to know how you did it, why you did it, so that we can help the next guy that's coming down the road, so we can stop it sooner, so there aren't five or 10 victims, so we can stop that guy after one."

And after a year of coming up with strategies, trying them on people, fine-tuning it, we got nothing from the guy. All he would say time and again was, "Yeah, but I didn't hurt anybody."

Kind of like John Wayne Gacy. Thirty-three bodies were found in the crawlspace under John Wayne Gacy's house in Chicago. I was starting [a prison interview] with Gacy and I said, "Hey, tell me about all those kids you buried in your crawl space." He said, "No I didn't, anybody could have done that. Anybody could have snuck up under my house and buried a kid."

RF: As one does. [*laughter*]

LM: I said, "OK, I'll give you one but I'm not giving you 33."

He was unhelpful also. Just like the South Side Strangler. He was not at all helpful. He didn't want to help us cut off this nonsense sooner. And I was surprised about that.

[Spencer] was quiet, deferential. He didn't look like a monster. You wouldn't pick him out of a crowd.

But we have had success with others and I was really hoping we would have success with this fellow, but it didn't happen.

RF: How did the South Side Strangler's M.O. fit the profile of serial killers? What sort of things do serial killers like him have in common?

LM: Well, one thing we noticed is that he was attacking the victims inside their residence and so Ray [Williams] started looking for burglars because they escalate. And sure enough he had escalated from burglary to sexual assault to murder. We invariably found a few dozen sexual assaults that he had committed, which means he may have committed 200 as a low number. Because ... so many of the victims do not report [rapes and sexual assaults]. So I look at 10 times the number that we find reported against one person as a ballpark number.

RF: That's pretty staggering.

LM: Once we had a handle on who he was, we were able to look back and see that escalating. One of the problems we had, though, is that statistically, Caucasians kill Caucasians and African-Americans kill other African-Americans. So we were looking for a white serial killer. The study of serial offenses was rather new at the time when this series was going on. If you look back exactly a hundred years previous, you would see Jack the Ripper as the prototypical serial killer and up until this time, we had always seen white, male serial killers. Well, this guy wasn't a white male and now we have female serial killers also.

RF: Anything else we might want to add? I think you've given us a lot.

LM: I'm about out of words. [*laughter*]

APPENDIX G: LOUIS SCHLESINGER INTERVIEW

This interview with Louis Schlesinger, Ph.D., a psychology professor and expert on serial killers from John Jay College of Criminal Justice in New York, was conducted in February 2018.

Richard Foster (RF): Dr. Schlesinger, can you tell me about yourself and your work in studying serial killers?

Louis Schlesinger (LS): I'm Dr. Louis Schlesinger, a professor of forensic psychology at John Jay College of Criminal Justice in New York and I've been a practicing forensic psychologist for 42 years and my area of expertise is murders and extraordinary crime, particularly sexually motivated murder.

RF: And you have experience studying serial killers, behavioral profiling?

LS: Yes. I wrote many books on this topic one of my books is entitled *Sexual Murder: Catathymic and Compulsive Homicides*, which involve different types of sexual murder, and I have a major research project with the FBI Behavioral Science Unit down at Quantico, where we've published some major papers on various aspects of serial sexual murder.

RF: So, looking about the Timothy Spencer case, this is a major milestone in forensic science and criminal law enforcement. Is this something that is taught in law enforcement education circles? Is this a case that's studied?

LS: Well, it's certainly studied by the FBI, that's for sure, because you know they handle a lot of serial sexual murder cases. ... But law enforcement in general? No, because the vast overwhelming majority of law enforcement officers are never going to see a serial sexual murder case. These are very rare cases. But those individuals who do handle this matter certainly study the Timothy Spencer case. It's a well-known case; it's an old case, over 30 years old. But, yes, it's still very relevant in many, many ways.

RF: Why is it still relevant today?

LS: Well, first of all ... it's important to understand what we're dealing with here: Timothy Spencer was a serial sexual murderer. ... The best way to understand serial sexual murder is to see it as an abnormal sexual arousal pattern that these people are not killing just because it's fun to do that and they want to do it, it's exceptionally arousing for them sexually. In these individuals there's a fusion of sex and aggression so that the aggressive act itself is eroticized and that's why that's the main motivation for them. And because it's so arousing for them, it's repetitive, it's compulsive and repetitive, and so you see a series of cases. That's fundamentally what the underlying problem is.

Now there's a couple of aspects of the Timothy Spencer case that are important to point out: One is that he was very aware forensically. He wore gloves during [his crimes]. ... Of course DNA wasn't an issue at the time and so he couldn't have been aware of it because nobody was really aware of it at that point. So that's an important aspect.

Also, prior to these murders and perhaps even during some of it, he engaged in sexually motivated burglary. The vast majority of burglaries are for gain, these are, you know, drug people or a group of people just want to steal money for personal reasons. But there's a subgroup of burglaries that are sexually motivated and there's two types of sexually motivated burglary: One is called fetish burglary, which law enforcement has been aware of for many years. It's when someone will get caught burglarizing and they're stealing women's underwear and this sort of thing shows the motivation for the burglary is overtly sexual. Because why would you just go into places to steal underwear? The more common type of sexual burglary is often missed by law enforcement and that's a voyeuristic burglary, where they have an urge to break in and look around and that's what voyeurism essentially is. The Boston Strangler, for example, engaged in voyeuristic burglary prior to killing. And the common denominator in many of the Boston Strangler crime scenes was the apartments are ransacked but nothing of value was taken. So anyway, in the Timothy Spencer case he had a history of burglary and these are sexually motivated. That's an important aspect of the case as well.

RF: And speaking of that, if you look at the pattern of the serial rapes that he committed, there's definitely an escalation in those that lead up to the first murder. Is that typical?

LS: Well, that doesn't occur in every case. Now many rapists, most rapists in fact, even serial rapists, don't go on to kill; some do. Some serial sexual murderers do not have a history of rape but some do. This is a case where he began with sexual burglary. It escalated to rape and then it escalated to sexual murder. Keep in mind, also, in terms of burglary, about 50 percent of burglaries occur in the evening when the occupants are likely to be home. So you can see how an escalation could [occur] when you break into a house and an occupant is there and then the victim becomes sexually assaulted and then a murder occurs. Also, with the Timothy Spencer case, he used a rape kit and I believe if my memory serves me correctly, [he used] some special types of knot that he was found to be using as well, which could help to link the number of different cases to him.

RF: One thing I don't really feel has been examined very much in this and that I really have not seen discussed is the bondage aspect. It seems like he got sexual gratification from not only the restraint but also from torturing these women. The medical examiner was telling me that the way that he had restrained them, it was essentially so that he could sort of take them to death's door and bring them back over and over.

LS: Exactly. Exactly. Spencer was a sexual sadist. He got sexual gratification from inflicting pain on others, but keep in mind, sadism, yes, it's the infliction of pain on someone else but more basic to the infliction of pain is so that the offender knows he is in complete control of the victim and that's what's most arousing. It's not just inflicting pain; it's controlling the person. So when he would strangle somebody as they were about to die, he would release the ligature so that they could come to and then continuing the strangling and in that way prolong the sadistic aggression and that is what is sexually arousing to him.

RF: Yeah, yeah it's pretty disturbing.

LS: Yeah, all these things are disturbing. You know, let me tell you one other aspect of this case, which I haven't looked at. We just published a paper, my group at John Jay and the FBI, on the temporal patterns in serial sexual murder. Most people have thought over the years that a serial sexual murderer will kill somebody and then deliberate for a period of time and then kill again and deliberate … trying to elude law enforcement and so on. That's not exactly true. Almost half of all serial sexual murderers occur in rapid sequence. Some kill all of their victims in one rapid-sequence, spree-like manner and another group kill in rapid-sequence clusters. So they kill one or two and then stop and three four or five and then stop. I'm not sure what the temporal patterns are in the Spencer case because I haven't looked at that.

RF: Yeah they're clusters, they're clusters.

LS: They're clusters. You see, there you go. There you go. If you want to look at it, you could look at my paper. It's called *Rapid-Sequence Serial Sexual Homicides* by myself and a group of others and was published in *The Journal of the American Academy of Psychiatry and Law* about a little bit less than a year ago. If you Google that, I guarantee you'll get the article.

RF: That's eerie because that's exactly what happened. They were in tight clusters.

LS: Yeah, that's very typical. And that's contrary to [what] most people think.

RF: Well, I remember, it seemed like the older theory was that they would kill on holidays or kill around certain times like a significant day or particular date or …

LS: Well that's all made up. … There's no scientific basis to that. What we do in my work, we've published empirical research on these cases. And so much of what you hear and learn about this from TV and the movies and so on is not based on peer empirical research; it's mostly speculation and people just referring to a couple of cases and that sort of thing. But we looked at, you know, I can't remember the exact number but close to 50 offenders and over 200 victims. So it's a pretty good sample, which we got from the FBI. It's a national sample.

RF: One thing I wanted to ask you with the escalation, near the end of his 1987 cluster of murders, he killed a 15-year-old high school student in her bedroom while her entire family was home. This was the first and only time he had ever committed an act like that with other people in the home and I would assume he had to know they were there because it seemed like he cased his targets pretty well. Do serial killers get more reckless, do they want to be caught?

LS: Well, they don't want to be caught, but they do get more reckless, particularly if they kill a number of people and don't get caught because they feel that they're going to outsmart law enforcement, law enforcement will never get them, that they're smarter than everybody. And so you often find that at the end of a killing cycle, they tend to get careless, they tend to get reckless. They do things not to get caught, they don't want to get caught, but they often do things to ensure that they _will_ get caught – like entering a home and raping and killing somebody while other family members are there or communicating with the police and sending them letters and this sort of thing. So that's not atypical at all.

RF: The defense attorney told me that even with them, Spencer was remarkably quiet, very taciturn. He barely said much of anything. Is that a typical thing, that somebody would be that withdrawn?

LS: No, it varies. It varies. You had Ted Bundy, who was in court representing himself, the same with Rodney Alcala, a lot of these guys want to go to court and represent themselves so that they can cross-examine family members and gain even more sadistic gratification in court, put a whole show on. On the other hand, some serial sexual murders just want to go to the cell and be left alone. It varies greatly.

RF: It's funny that you should mention the gratification in court. The one story that I've been told and the prosecution, defense, witnesses, they all say this. They said the only time they saw any reaction from Spencer in court was during the first trial when he saw pictures of the victim and everyone said he seemed to be taking a real interest in those photos.

LS: Well, what happens in some cases is, after the case is over and the person is in state prison, the offender will get the crime scene photos. And he's saying, well, I need this because I'm working on my appeal and basically you have to give it to him. It's part of the case.

But they're not doing it to work on their appeal. They're using the crime scene photos as a form of pornography, to re-live the crime in their own fantasy.

RF: Wow, yeah, I've never heard of that. That's pretty harsh. I also wanted to ask you about the evolution of behavioral profiling. At the time this case this happened in late 1987, the notion of behavioral profiling, that whole science was still fairly new at that point, right?

LS: Yes, yes basically. ... These things have certainly evolved in a very significant way. And they were just trying to understand what was going on at that time and things are very, very different now in the use of behavioral analysis and crime scene analysis. The FBI is very good at that. They have a lot of experience and they do a very, very good job. But the one thing to remember with behavioral analysis and so on, you know, it got overhyped a lot, particularly in the early '90s with *The Silence of the Lambs* and this sort of thing and, you know, it's an adjunct to police work and never should take the place of police work and certainly the FBI folks know that. But sometimes you hear in the media, you know, the profilers are on their way, they'll have a profile, all sorts of nonsense like that. It's an adjunct of technique and the FBI folks that use this are very, very good at it. There are up on all the science, not just the lore.

RF: What I've been told from some of the people on the law enforcement side is that at that time there was a profile that was put together by behavioral profilers based on the killings in Richmond. They didn't yet realize the killings were connected to the ones in Arlington. But they were looking for a white man, not a black killer, because they didn't think that serial killers were typically black.

LS: The old notion was that serial sexual murderers are predominantly white. That's not true. African-Americans are well represented among the group of serial sexual murderers. So are all races for that matter, Asian individuals ... [There are] serial sexual murders in every country, in every culture and from pre-modern times. These cases have been documented back in the 1800s. If you take a look at Richard von Krafft-Ebing's [book] *Psychopathia Sexualis*, it discusses cases back in the 1800s of serial sexual murder. But you know back in the 1980s people that were doing this at the time were going by what they knew and what they thought was correct. That shouldn't be considered a criticism. It's the development of the method, the development of science, the development of a technique. You know, people in medicine thought a lot of things that hat were done as a general practice of medicine … [that] now it turns out that that wasn't really correct. It's not a criticism. They're doing what they thought was correct at the time and that's the nature of science, we're learning a lot more now. Look at the temporal patterns: Our study is the first empirical examination of the temporal patterns [in] serial sexual murder. It's never been done before. And so people looked at this not carelessly but just thought about it and got a wrong impression.

RF: My thinking is they were only interviewing white serial killers and I think part of the reason they were is because, this is my theory and tell me if I'm way off, but I think in the '60s, '70s, maybe even in the '80s, you know, there's still a lot of racial bias in law enforcement. And while it's kind of ironic because more blacks were locked up, especially in the Southern states, you probably had a situation where the murder of a black woman probably wouldn't have gotten the same attention by police as the murder of a white victim at the same time.

LS: That is true, that's certainly true and you know I'm sure that's true. But again, they're going by what they thought was correct. And so at that time when they started this back in the '70s actually, behavioral profiling and behavioral analysis, they were studying cases that were out there at the time, the Boston Strangler was the case [study]. Jack the Ripper was the case [study]. William Heirens, the Chicago [Lipstick Killer] case and they're all white. And so after you

219

studied maybe 20 of these, you get the idea that maybe this is just a white person's thing, [but] that's not true at all. But that's what was thought then. Again, as science develops, as more experience is gained and when empirical research is done, then we learn more about it.

RF: I think it's just data collection and it was the evolution of it. The other thing I want to point out was the fact that this was a very new concept, I mean the concept of behavioral profiling really didn't exist until, what, 1975?

LS: Yes, yes, that's correct. And then in the early to mid '70s they just began doing it. It was around '86, '88, I think, that the FBI first started publishing some articles on this. And then it was only a few groups, only a few people doing this, you know, in the FBI, no more than three or four or five people. So, you know, you've got to give a lot of credit to the early folks doing this, but you can't hold them to today's standards of 2018, what they were doing in the mid '70s. We learned. As you gain experience, you'll learn. And then you change your methods, change your techniques and we're continuing to learn as well. I published another study in the same journal, *The Journal American Academy of Psychiatry and Law* titled *Ritual and Signature in Serial Sexual Homicide*. You might want to take a look at that because again we did empirical research on what these guys do signature-wise and ritualistically at various crime scenes. It's a lot different than what you see on TV. You know, they're not putting butterflies in the mouth like in *Silence of the Lambs*. It's very different, but that's what people thought you know was true.

RF: Well sure. I mean that's all we saw about on TV and in the movies and the media back then.

LS: Exactly.

RF: So what is what is the truth? What is the truth more likely to be in terms of ritual?

LS: Well, it's much more complicated. But I tell you, what I consider the most important finding that we found ... that was published in 2010, I think. The most important finding is experimentation at a crime scene. If you look at serial killers ... very often ... in 70 percent of the cases the offender will do something with one victim in a series that he did not do with the other four, so let's say for example there's five victims, four of them, they're left nude, dumped. One of them, their breasts are cut off, you know, or their eyes are cut out, or, you know, they're posed with foreign object insertions. When the average homicide detective looks at that, even with 25 years experience, he or she may never have had a serial sexual murder case. So when you look at it common sense being what it is, you would say the perp, the one with the eyes cut out or the breast cut off or something shoved up them, it's got to be a different offender because it looks so different than the others in that series that are linked. [But] it's not true. When you look at a large number of them like we did, in 70 percent of the cases, one victim is handled very, very differently and ... they experiment with one victim. We also looked at [whether] experimentation occurs in the middle, in the end or in the beginning. And we found out it's equal, you know, as far as we can determine. It's very interesting. As we study it, we're learning more.

RF: How unusual is it for a serial killer to commit murders in two cities a hundred miles apart, like the South Side Strangler did?

LS: Well, most serial murderers, like most criminals, commit crimes where they're comfortable, and they gain comfort from familiar surroundings, where they live, where they work, where they visited and so on. So, again, if you look at serial killers, even very prolific serial killers, most of the murders occur in one geographic area because that's where they're comfortable. Now there are cases where there's two comfort zones. Say the person lives and works in this area, but he may have previously lived in another area or has relatives there that he visited. So now in this particular case Spencer, it was a 100-mile area where these occurred [and] that's fairly rare unless Spencer had comfort in both of these locations. I don't know if he did it or not. I just don't remember that aspect.

RF: He did; he did.

LS: There you go, that's the answer to that.

ABOUT THE AUTHOR

While he was still a college journalism student, award-winning writer Richard Foster became the first reporter to track down and interview the legendary, reclusive pin-up model Bettie Page. His 1997 biography of her, *The Real Bettie Page*, was adapted into the 2006 HBO film *The Notorious Bettie Page*. Foster has written and edited for numerous magazines and newspapers over the last 25 years. Most recently, he hosted the true-crime podcast series *Southern Nightmare: The Hunt for the South Side Strangler*. Foster, who has two adult sons, lives with his wife, Miriam, in Richmond, Virginia, with their four very needy cats.

INDEX

and Timothy Spencer, 87, 94, 143-45

links to Tucker murder, 62-64, 69, 79-80

and Vasquez arrest, 69, 76, 140

Han, Jenny, 37, 42-45, 47-48, 52, 56-57

Harrington, Morgan, 156

Harvey family murders (Bryan, Kathryn, Ruby and Stella), 32

Hayes, Ronald, 89-90, 107

Henry, Darla, 132-33, 136

Hellams, Dr. Susan

autopsy, 29

body found, 19

and Cloverleaf Mall, 33

community reaction to murder, 30-32

and DNA, 104, 105, 109

early life, 19

and husband, 18, 21

last seen alive, 23-24

and Medical College of Virginia, 19-22, 90

murder investigation, 24-25, 27-28, 30, 32-33, 79-80

murder trial, 123-24

and other South Side Strangler victims, 24-25, 32, 49, 51, 79, 81, 85, 88, 90

Horgas, Joe

arrest of Timothy Spencer, 99-102, 195-200

and DNA testing, 105, 109, 198

and FBI Behavioral Science Unit, 82-83, 85, 194-95

and Hamm murder, 63, 78-79

and interrogation of Timothy Spencer, 102-03, 195-97, 200

RICHARD FOSTER